Poems
Teacher's Book

Introduction

'What the child, and the child-in-the-adult, most enjoys in poetry
. . . is the manipulation of language for its own sake, the sound and
rhythm of words.' W. H. Auden, Introduction to *A Choice of de la
Mare's Verse* (Faber, 1963)

'We can sum up by saying that whatever else the pupil takes away
from his experience of literature in school he should have learned
to see it as a source of pleasure, as something that will continue to
be part of his life.' Bullock Report, *A Language for Life* (HMSO,
1975)

'Everyone is a poet who can dance in time to a band at a party or
march in step on parade. Poetry is the shortest way of saying
things. It also looks nicer on the page than prose. It gives room to
think and dream.' Sir John Betjeman, *The New Dragon Book of Verse*
(OUP, 1977)

Poems is the first book in a poetry teaching course. The course hopes to develop an enjoyment of poetry that will last. We believe that to enjoy poetry you have to understand something of how it works. *Poems* can be seen as a linking book between the children's existing experience and the main body of English poetry.

Poetry involves playing with words. We set out to show children that they already have some experience of poetry because they are used to word-play and rhythm in jokes, riddles, and playground rhymes. Our selection of these is not original because we start with what is known, familiar, and secure.

From this familiar ground we move gently to simple poems. The emphasis is still on the fun to be had with words and rhythms. We then move gradually to the stage where the reader needs to work at a poem. By this stage he should be convinced that poetry is on his side. Simple fun should be giving way to subtler and more lasting pleasures – but the pleasures must be there.

The Teacher's Book provides four ways into a poem. Children who have worked through the course will gradually have acquired a routine that will help them approach a poem. In *Poems* we signpost one of these ways for each poem:

Story: What is the poem about?
Some poems tell simple incidents and others tell full stories. In
later books we see how poems can be 'about' a huge variety of
subjects. In *Poems* we use this signpost for poems that tell a fairly
straightforward story.

Feeling: What feelings does the poem evoke in us?
Poems are used to explore and to record feelings such as
excitement, terror, joy, love, happiness. The feelings themselves
can be considered separately from the way in which they are
evoked. Poems used must be related to the feelings the reader has
experienced.

Pattern: How are the words of the poem arranged?
In poems, as in other art forms, we look for some regularity or
repetition. It can come from rhyme, rhythm, or the shape of the
words on the page.

Image: What pictures does the poem create in our minds?
In *Poems* we start with riddles as examples of how words can create
pictures. Descriptive poems and examples of simile and metaphor
show the visual and aural presentation of imagery.

In the notes on the poems, we pick out and concentrate on one of
these ways. But the other ways are always relevant; sometimes we
draw attention to these in the work we have suggested.

D

A Teacher's page is in three sections:

Section 1 has comments for the teacher about the poem: it explains why the poem is included where it is and highlights which of the four approaches is intended as the main one. The language in this section is geared to the teacher.

Section 2 consists of questions for the class. Some or all of these may be read out for discussion or used as the basis for written answers. The language in this section is geared to the child.

Section 3 contains follow-up work, with cross-references to other poems in the book and to other anthologies (*JV = Junior Voices; NDBV = New Dragon Book of Verse*).

All the anthologies mentioned are available in paperback. The four volumes of *Junior Voices* are referred to regularly: these are, we feel, books which all children should have the opportunity to meet. If sets of *Junior Voices* are available, they will make it easier to use this book fully.

The teacher's material concentrates on the content and structure of the particular poem. Only in a few cases have we used the poem as a stimulus for the children's own writing; this we call the 'centrifugal' approach to contrast it with the 'centripetal' emphasis on the text of the poem. The poems may, of course, all be used as a stimulus for writing, art, or drama, but it is much more important that they are enjoyed for themselves.

We want to stress that pupils will certainly benefit simply by reading through a poem and enjoying it. Sometimes there is no need to do anything else. To work through the book from cover to cover, using all the teacher's material, would be monotonous. We hope that the teacher will be flexible and selective in the use he makes of our comments, questions, cross-references, and follow-up poems.

E

How to use this book

The Standard Lesson Pattern: READ DISCUSS READ

The teacher reads the poem while the pupils have the anthology either open or shut (see second paragraph opposite). He may want to read it more than once or, occasionally, to get a pupil to read it.

Read out the first question for class discussion (see third paragraph opposite). Move on to the next question when it seems right.

Finally, either the teacher or pupils (or both) read the poem again.

Some of the follow-up work on the opposite page can be used.

Three variations

1 Instead of having class discussion, split up for group discussion.

The groups can report back.

End with each group, or some of the groups, reading to the class.

2 The questions can be used for written answers by being read out, written on the blackboard, or reproduced. This can be a preliminary to discussion.

3 We repeat: please don't stick to the same lesson format to the point of boredom. Have some lessons that are just reading poems for pure enjoyment.

F

We believe there are two very important points about teaching poetry:

All poetry is written primarily to be heard. We hope that any introduction to a poem will start with the teacher reading the poem to the class. The teacher may choose whether to make any preliminary remarks before reading and whether to have the class following in the book or not. Many of the poems have an element of surprise in them. You can keep this sense of surprise by letting the pupils hear the poem first, and see it later. A class discussion can then follow, along the lines suggested in 'How to Use this Book'. After the discussion the class should read the poem aloud, either in groups or individually. The pupils should now be able to comprehend the poem more fully and should read the poem aloud with more understanding.

In all discussion on a poem it is important to lead back into the poem. There is a natural 'centrifugal' tendency to talk about one's own experience at the expense of the poem. Keep asking for supporting evidence *from the text of the poem itself.*

Follow-up work

Note: Some of this section is what we have described as **centrifugal:** leading away from the poem. These activities will normally follow the Standard Lesson although, for variation's sake, they will sometimes form the complete lesson.

1   Use the poem as a starting-point for pupils' writing.
2   Ask the pupils to collect poems that will go with the lesson poem in some way.
3   Over the year pupils can make a personal anthology of poems and lines from poems that they like. These can be illustrated.
4   Pupils can be encouraged to learn by heart poems and lines from poems that they like.
5   Pupils present their anthologies to the class, individually or in groups. These can be read out, written and displayed, or tape-recorded.
6   Some poems will lead naturally into drama.
7   At the end of term, or of the year, hold a request programme of favourite poems.
8   Make full use of BBC broadcasts to add variety and stimulus, especially *Living Language* and *Listening and Writing.*

G

Themes

We have provided a list of themes (p. L) for those who wish to integrate poetry into topic work, rather than to follow this book through from the beginning to the end. The relevant teacher's pages will lead to similar poems in *Junior Voices*. For further poems see Morris: *Where's That Poem?* (Basil Blackwell).

Haiku

We have included five haiku from Anthony Thwaite's *Haiku Calendar*, where they fit into a theme. Haiku is a Japanese verse form originally consisting of three lines of 5, 7, and 5 syllables each. This is supposed to be the optimum length for one breath. They usually present one clear image, and provide good models for imitation. The complete Haiku Calendar follows here:

Snow in January
Looking for ledges
To hide in unmelted.

February evening:
A cold puddle of petrol
Makes its own rainbow.

Wind in March:
No leaves left
For its stiff summons.

April sunlight:
Even the livid bricks
Muted a little.

Wasp in May
Storing his venom
For a long summer.

Morning in June:
On the sea's horizon
A white island, alone.

July evening:
Sour reek of beer
Warm by the river.

August morning:
A squirrel leaps and
Only one branch moves.

September chestnuts:
Falling too early,
Split white before birth.

October garden:
At the top of the tree
A thrush stabs an apple.

November morning:
A whiff of cordite
Caught in the leaf mould.

Sun in December:
In his box of straw
The tortoise wakes.

Anthony Thwaite, Inscriptions (OUP)

Bibliography

1 Books for the teacher on teaching poetry

Douglas Barnes: *From Communication to Curriculum* (Penguin)
An essential examination of the problems of discussion in class.
Michael Marland: *The Craft of the Classroom* (Heinemann Educational)
Covers the practical problems thoroughly and sensibly.
I. A. Richards: *Practical Criticism* (Routledge and Kegan Paul)
Examines the difficulties in talking about poetry, with some suggestions
for practice.
Frank Whitehead: *The Disappearing Dais* (Chatto and Windus)
Useful advice on the 'centripetal' approach.

2 An invaluable reference book

Helen Morris: *Where's That Poem?* (Basil Blackwell)
Lists of poems arranged by themes.

3 Some relevant hardback poetry books for the teacher

Charles Causley: *Collected Poems* (Macmillan)
Ted Hughes: *Moon-Bells and Other Poems* (Chatto and Windus)
The Earth-Owl (Faber and Faber)
Season Songs (Faber and Faber)
Michael Rosen: *Wouldn't You Like to Know* (André Deutsch)

4 Books for the class library, all paperbacks

Hilaire Belloc: *Selected Cautionary Verses* (Puffin)
Charles Causley: *The Puffin Book of Magic Verse* (Puffin)
Charles Causley: *The Puffin Book of Salt-Sea Verse* (Puffin)
David Davis: *A Single Star* (Puffin)
Robert Froman: *Seeing Things* (Abelard Grasshopper)
Eleanor Graham: *A Puffin Quartet of Poets* (Puffin)
Michael Harrison and Christopher Stuart-Clark: *The New Dragon Book of
Verse* (OUP)
Ted Hughes: *Meet My Folks* (Puffin)
David Jackson: *Ways of Talking* (Ward Lock Educational)
Michael Rosen: *Mind Your Own Business* (Armada Lions)
Dennis Saunders: *Hist Whist* (Piccolo)
Dennis Saunders and Vincent Oliver: *Poems and Pictures series* (Evans)
Ian Serraillier: *I'll Tell You a Tale* (Puffin)
Geoffrey Summerfield: *Junior Voices I–IV* (Penguin)
Julia Watson: *A Children's Zoo* (Armada Lions)
Kit Wright: *Rabbiting On and Other Poems* (Fontana Lions)

J

K

Themes

M

N

Acknowledgements

The Editors gratefully acknowledge permission to reprint the following copyright material:

Daniel Abse: From *The Tenants of the House* (Hutchinson Publishing Company) Reprinted by permission of Anthony Sheil Associates Ltd. **Charles Causley:** From *Collected Poems of Charles Causley* (Macmillan, London and Basingstoke). Reprinted by permission of David Higham Associates Ltd. **Kevin Crossley-Holland:** From *The Rain Giver* (1972). Reprinted by permission of André Deutsch Ltd. **e. e. cummings:** From *Collected Poems, 1913–1962*. Reprinted by permission of Granada Publishing Ltd. **Ronald Deadman:** From *Words in your Ear*. Reprinted by permission of Evans Brothers Ltd. **Walter de la Mare:** From *The Complete Poems of de la Mare 1969* (Faber & Faber Ltd.). Reprinted by permission of the Literary Trustees of the Estate of Walter de la Mare and The Society of Authors as their representative. **Eleanor Farjeon:** From *Silver, Sand and Snow* (Michael Joseph Ltd.). Reprinted by permission of David Higham Associates Ltd. **Robert Froman:** From *Seeing Things* (Grasshopper Books, 1977). Reprinted by permission of Abelard-Schuman Ltd. **Robert Frost:** From *The Poetry of Robert Frost*, edited by Edward Connery Lathem. Reprinted by permission of the Estate of Robert Frost and Jonathan Cape Ltd. **Roy Fuller:** 'You can tell how wound up I am', 'Full, over-full is my heart', 'End of a Girl's First Tooth', 'The Dark', 'Be a Monster', 'The Game of Life' from *Poor Roy* (1977). Reprinted by permission of André Deutsch Ltd. 'Horrible Things', 'TV' from *Seen Grandpa Lately?* Reprinted by permission of André Deutsch Ltd. **Robert Graves:** From *Collected Poems of Robert Graves* (Cassell & Co. Ltd.). Reprinted by permission of A. P. Watt & Son on behalf of Mr. Robert Graves. **John Heath-Stubbs:** From *A Charm Against Toothache* (Oxford University Press). Reprinted by permission of David Higham Associates Ltd. **Russell Hoban:** From *The Pedalling Man*. Reprinted by permission of World's Work Ltd. **Ralph Hodgson:** From *Collected Poems of Ralph Hodgson*. Reprinted by permission of Mrs. Hodgson, and Macmillan, London and Basingstoke. **Ted Hughes:** 'Moon-Wind', 'Horrible Song' from *Moon Bells*. Reprinted by permission of Faber & Faber Ltd. and Chatto & Windus Ltd. 'My Father' from *Meet my Folks*. Reprinted by permission of Faber & Faber Ltd. **Pat Hutchins:** From *Don't Forget the Bacon*. Reprinted by permission of The Bodley Head. **Brian Jones:** From *The Spitfire on the Northern Line*. © Brian Jones 1975. Reprinted by permission of Chatto & Windus Ltd. **Philip Larkin:** From *The Whitsun Weddings*. Reprinted by permission of Faber & Faber Ltd. **Brian Lee:** From *Late Home* (Kestrel Books, 1976). © Brian Lee 1976. Reprinted by permission of Penguin Books Ltd. **J. A. Lindon:** From *As Large as Alone: Recent Poems*, edited by Christopher Copeman and James Gibson (Macmillan, London and Basingstoke). Reprinted by permission of the author. **Marian Lines:** From *Tower Blocks*. Reprinted by permission of Franklin Watts Ltd. **Tom Lowenstein** (trans.): From *Eskimo Poems from Canada and Greenland*. Reprinted by permission of Allison & Busby Ltd. **Charles Malam:** From *Upper Pasture*. Copyright 1930, © Charles Malam 1950. Reprinted by permission of Holt, Rinehart and Winston, Inc. Publishers. **Gerda Mayer:** From *The Knockabout Show*. © Gerda Mayer 1978. Reprinted by permission of Chatto & Windus Ltd. **Roger McGough:** From *In the Glassroom* (Jonathan Cape). © Roger McGough 1976. Reprinted by permission of Hope

Leresche & Sayle. **Edwin Morgan:** From *Concrete Poetry*, edited by Stephen Bann. Copyright London Magazine Editions 1967. Reprinted by permission.
Brian Patten: From *The Sly Cormorant and the Fishes* (Kestrel Books, 1977) © Brian Patten 1977. Reprinted by permission of Penguin Books Ltd. **James Reeves:** From *The Collected Poems of James Reeves*. Reprinted by permission of Heineman Educational Books Ltd. **Theodore Roethke:** From *The Collected Poems of Theodore Roethke*. Reprinted by permission of Faber & Faber Ltd. **Michael Rosen:** 'My Dad's Thumb', 'Father Says', 'In the Daytime' from *Mind Your Own Business* (1974). Reprinted by permission of André Deutsch Ltd. 'I'm Just Going Out For a Moment' from *Wouldn't You Like to Know* (1977). Reprinted by permission of André Deutsch Ltd. **Carl Sandburg:** 'Portrait of a Motor Car' ('It's a Lean Car') from *Cornhuskers*. Copyright 1918 Holt, Rinehart and Winston, Inc., copyright 1964 Carl Sandburg. Reprinted by permission of Harcourt Brace Janovich, Inc. 'Sea Wash' from *Smoke and Steel*. Copyright 1902 Harcourt Brace Jovanovich, Inc., copyright 1948 Carl Sandburg. Reprinted by permission of the publisher.
Vernon Scannell: From *Apple Raid* (Chatto Poets for the Young). Reprinted by permission of the author. **Ian Serraillier:** From *After Ever Happily* (Oxford University Press). © Ian Serrailler 1963. Reprinted by permission of the author. **Gertrude Stein:** From *My Kind of Verse* (Burke Publishing Co. Ltd.). Reprinted by permission of David Higham Associates Ltd. **L. A. G. Strong:** From *The Body's Imperfections*. Reprinted by permission of Methuen & Co. Ltd. **Hal Summers:** From *Tomorrow is my Love*. Reprinted by permission of the author and Oxford University Press. **R. S. Thomas:** From *Song at the Year's Turning*. Reprinted by permission of Granada Publishing Ltd. **Anthony Thwaite:** From *Inscriptions*. Reprinted by permission of the author and Oxford University Press.
J. R. R. Tolkien: 'Washing up Song' from *The Hobbit*. Reprinted by permission of George Allen & Unwin (Publishers) Ltd. **Judith Wright:** From *Collected Poems: 1942–1970*. Reprinted by permission of Angus & Robertson Publishers.
Kit Wright: From *Rabbiting On*. Reprinted by permission of Wm. Collins & Sons Co. Ltd. **Andrew Young:** From *Andrew Young's Complete Poems*, edited by Leonard Clark. Reprinted by permission of Martin Secker & Warburg Ltd.

The publishers would like to thank the following for permission to reproduce photographs:

Barnaby's Picture Library: 4, 36, 37, 54, 57, 73, 74/75, 88; Janet and Colin Bord: 62; Lance Browne: 1, 5, 19, 20/21, 25, 31, 32, 38, 41, 53, 66/67, 94; Bruce Coleman: 34; Gwynedd Archives Service: 51; Hills Harris: 22/23, 28/29, 84/85; Institute of Geological Sciences (Crown Copyright): 44; Oxford Scientific Films: 69, 70; Royal Astronomical Society (photo: Hale Observatories): 58; Bill Eglon Shaw (photo: Frank Meadow Sutcliffe): 79.

Cover design by Jeffrey Tabberner

Finally we should like to acknowledge our indebtedness to Ron Heapy, of the Oxford University Press, for his help and encouragement in the preparation of this book and to Rita Winstanley and Alison Souster, also of the University Press, for their co-operation and imagination in its design.

Oxford, 1979   M. J. H., C. A. S-C.

P

Poems

edited by

Michael Harrison and
Christopher Stuart-Clark

Oxford University Press

Contents

Can an elephant jump higher than a lamp-post?
    Yes, lamp-posts can't jump.

Why do elephants have big ears?
    Noddy wouldn't pay the ransom.

Why do elephants paint the soles of their feet yellow?
    So they can hide upside down in the custard.
Have you ever seen an elephant hiding upside-down
    in the custard?
    No.
Shows what a good disguise it is.

How can you tell if
there's an elephant in the refrigerator?
    You can't shut the door.

How can you tell if
an elephant has been in your fridge?
    Footprints in the butter.

Although jokes are not poetry, there are similarities which can make them useful as a 'way in' to **pattern.**

Jokes are brief except for the shaggy-dog story, which works because jokes are usually brief. They use a minimum of words: this teaches that poetry is compressed language.

Jokes spring partly from a delight in words and their ambiguities; here the 'big ears' joke and the lamp-post joke involve puns on words like 'big ears' and 'jump higher'. The double meaning of words creates jokes, e.g. Two flies playing football in a saucer, and one says 'We must practise hard, next week we're playing in the cup.' Poetry also delights in and exploits words.

Jokes are not suitable for analysis and detailed discussion, but the class can swop examples and make their own anthologies. However jokes often rely on double meanings or are just obscene. Be careful that the lesson doesn't get out of hand.

Do you know any other 'elephant' jokes?

Do you know any 'fly in the soup' jokes?

What is the best joke you have heard recently? What actually made it funny?

Can you think of any advertisements which play with words?

Make up slogans or advertisements for some incredible causes, e.g.

The Pet Mouse in every Home Campaign, The Anti-Corn Flakes League, The No-School-on-Mondays Movement.

More jokes can be found in: *The Puffin Crack-a-Joke Book* and *The Puffin Joke Book.*

See also the word-play in: *Ice Cream Poem, Girl's First Tooth.* (p. 19.)

Jokes tend to have a definite **pattern**: this is particularly true of 'Knock Knock' jokes. The 'Granny' joke here exploits the pattern. Poetry could almost be defined as patterned words.

   Ask pairs of pupils to read out the jokes on this page, as these jokes have to be *heard*. These are classic 'puns', which depend on the play on sound for their effect (as in the butcher's slogan, 'Pleased to meet you, Meat to please you').

Make up a Knock Knock joke for your first-name.

Write down several Knock Knock jokes you know. Which ones work easily and well, which ones do not?

Do you know any joke book titles, such as Death on the Cliff *by Eileen Dover?*

Do you know any really suitable nicknames for certain people?

Make up some suitable nicknames for: a judge; a traffic-warden; a chemistry teacher; an air-hostess; a space-man; a skater.

Think of some other nicknames from your own ideas.

There are more Knock Knock jokes in *The Puffin Crack-a-Joke Book* and *JV* IV: 1.

   The pattern of conversation established in these jokes is only extended a little in *Why?* by Michael Rosen and *Rabbiting On* by Kit Wright (pp. 16, 17).

Knock, knock.
Who's there?
Ivor
Ivor who?
Ivor you let me in the door or I'll climb in the window.

Knock, knock.
Who's there?
Olive
Olive who?
Olive here, so let me in!

Knock, knock.
Who's there?
Luke
Luke who?
Luke through the keyhole and you'll see.

Knock, knock.
Who's there?
Granny.
Knock, knock.
Who's there?
Granny.
Knock, knock.
Who's there?
Granny.
Knock, knock.
Who's there?
Aunt.
Aunt who?
Aunt you glad I got rid of all those grannies?

Knock, knock.
Who's there?
Arfer
Arfer who?
Arfer got.

Knock, knock.
Who's there?
Ken
Ken who?
Ken I come in?

5

Cry baby, cry,
Punch him in the eye,
Hang him on the lamp-post
And leave him there to dry.

If you stay to school dinners
Better throw them aside,
A lot of kids didn't,
A lot of kids died.
The meat is of iron.
The spuds are of steel,
If that don't get you
Then the afters will.

Sir is kind and sir is gentle
Sir is strong and sir is mental.

For what we have put back on the dish
May the school chickens be truly grateful.

For what we have put back on the dish
May second dinner be truly grateful.

Tell tale tit,
Your tongue shall be slit,
And all the dogs in the town
Shall have a little bit.

Jokes are based on a recognizable **pattern**; and this is half their appeal. So, if children are presented with a ready-made pattern they will enjoy being inventive within it. For example, consider the various versions of 'Happy Birthday to You' and 'While shepherds watched'.

On this page the second chant is based on a well-known song, and the fourth and fifth on a grace.

The other three chants arise from particular situations, and have a good, simple **rhythm** to them: there are several versions and many similar playground chants.

Read out 'If you stay. . .', clapping or stamping to the rhythm.

Do you know any well-known songs with words rewritten, like this one? How about Happy Birthday to You, While shepherds watched, John Brown's Body, Land of Hope and Glory?

Do you know any other rhymes about food?

Cry, baby, cry *and* Tell tale tit *are chanted at other people. Can you think of any others, or different versions of these?*

Do you know any other rhymes about teachers or school? About the end of term, for example.

Do you know any counting rhymes, e.g. Tinker, Tailor, Soldier, Sailor?

Do you know any chants that are shouted at football matches?

There will probably be a fund of examples of this sort of rhyming from the children themselves, but the Opies' *Lore and Language of Schoolchildren* (O.U.P.) has plenty of further examples.

More chants: *JV I:6 Order in Court/Through the Teeth; JV III:32 Step on a Crack; JV III:53 Teacher, teacher.*

Queen Nefertiti has a strong and easily recognizable **rhythm**. Read it to the class, emphasizing the beat, then ask them to read it together, clapping the rhythm at the same time.

This can be used as a counting-out **rhyme**, using the beats as numbers like 'Eeny, meeny,' etc

---

If you are counting people out to the rhyme, Queen Nefertiti, *how many could you count out each verse?*

Do you know any other counting-out rhymes, e.g. Eena, meena, mina, mo?

Further examples of counting-out rhymes are in *Lore and Language of Schoolchildren* and in *Junior Voices I*: 80–81.

See also:

The Minister in the Pulpit JV I:19
Salt, Mustard (another counting-out rhyme) *JV* I:76
Skip to my Lou JV I:56.

Queen Nefertiti

Spin a coin, spin a coin,
   All fall down;
Queen Nefertiti
   Stalks through the town.

Over the pavements
   Her feet go clack.
Her legs are as tall
   As a chimney stack;

Her fingers flicker
   Like snakes in the air,
The walls split open
   At her green-eyed stare;

Her voice is thin
   As the ghosts of bees;
She will crumble your bones
   She will make your blood freeze.

Spin a coin, spin a coin,
   All fall down,
Queen Nefertiti
   Stalks through the town.

Anon

Four stiff standers
Four dilly danders
Two lookers
Two crookers
And a wig-wag.

Two brothers we are
Great burdens we bear
On which we are bitterly pressed;
The truth is to say
We are full all the day
And empty when we go to rest.

Little Nancy Etticoat
With a white petticoat
And a red nose;
She has no feet or hands
The longer she stands
The shorter she grows.

He went to the wood and caught it
He sat him down and sought it;
Because he could not find it,
Home with him he brought it.

8

There is a close connection between puzzle-jokes (like 'Why do elephants have big ears?' on p. 4 and 'What is orange and comes out of the ground at 100 m.p.h.?; an E-type carrot') and more traditional riddles. Riddles are playing with words, using **pattern** with words and also using words to disguise meanings, by giving plenty of detail but not the straight answer. The riddles on this page are traditional ones (A: a cow; B: pair of shoes; C: a candle; D: a flea). An understanding of this use of words will help children to understand **imagery** in poetry later on.

Ask certain pupils to read out these riddles, and then get them to work out the answers, either in groups or by themselves.

Do you know any other riddles? Find some more in Junior Voices.
There are more riddles on pp. 22–23. Read them and work them out.
Write your own riddles for:
a chimney, a rainbow, teeth, a hedgehog, ice, a wheelbarrow, the moon.

There are plenty of riddles in *Junior Voices*: JV I:47. II:1. III:2,4. IV:1, 76. If the class has managed pp. 22–23 well, go on to p. 24, and consider *Fire* and *Haystack*.

Old Mrs. Lazibones appeals because it deals with laziness and dirt, uses an original and unexpected chorus involving 'cowpat', and has an easy rhythm. Read it out to the class, bringing out the beat.

While Queen Nefertiti was a mysterious character, Mrs. Lazibones is just dirty. Arrange a reading of the poem, with different pupils taking the verses and all chanting the chorus each time.

This poem tells a simple **story** rather than just being a chant, and is an introduction to the ballad. It also points a moral.

This poem tells a simple story; what actually happens in the story?

What does this poem suggest we might learn from what happened to Mrs. Lazibones' daughter?

Do you know any other rhymes or songs with choruses which are repeated like 'Higgledy-piggledy cowpat?' For example, Glory, Glory, Hallelujah?

For another character of strange appearance, read
    All Dressed Up JV I:14.
For further choruses, compare:
    Old Roger is dead JV I:23
    Praise Song of the Wind JV II:21
    Rattlesnake JV II:44
    The Big Rock Candy Mountains NDBV:112
    Two Old Women of Mumbling Hill p. 26.

Old Mrs Lazibones

Old Mrs Lazibones
And her dirty daughter
Never used soap
And never used water.
    Higgledy piggledy cowpat
    What d'you think of that?

Daisies from their fingernails,
Birds' nests in their hair-O,
Dandelions from their ears, —
What a dirty pair-O!
    Higgledy piggledy cowpat
    What d'you think of that?

Came a prince who sought a bride,
Riding past their doorstep,
Quick, said Mrs Lazibones.
Girl, under the watertap.
    Higgledy piggledy cowpat
    What d'you think of that?

Washed her up and washed her down,
Then she washed her sideways,
But the prince was far, far away,
He'd ridden off on the highways.
    Higgledy piggledy cowpat
    What d'you think of that?

Gerda Mayer

9

Through

beside

Around

bove

Between

Under

neath

10

The pattern of words has been seen in jokes and catchy chants. It is also possible to give the words a visual **pattern** to help convey their full meaning. One way of encouraging children to look for more than the basic, obvious use of a word is to consider 'word-shapes', which use more than a sequence of letters and sound.

The visual impact of this page should mean that little introduction is required by the teacher, apart from encouraging the children to experiment.

Which of the words do you think is the best?

Try to improve on these: one group work on ABOVE, another on THROUGH and so on, doing your own 'shape versions' of the words.

Now try with some new words. Choose one of the following words and draw your own shape with the letters:
crooked, tall, church, sinking, splash, banana, rocket, shout, corn-flakes. Pass the various word-shapes around in groups and choose the best in each group.

Now think of some new words of your own to experiment with. When you have finished, pass them around your group and choose the best ones for display in the classroom. Do your own as neatly as you can in your writing book.

The idea of words, etc. having characters or personalities is continued in *Apostrophe* by Roger McGough and *AEIOU* by Jonathan Swift (pp. 18 and 23).

After building single images with single words, it is possible to make more complex **pictures** with whole sentences and whole ideas. This picture and the two following pages illustrate this.

   Weekend in the Country uses a variety of single words to give a picture and to convey a 'message' about the parallel roads.

What is this a picture of?

What different things are causing the different sounds shown?

What is the point of the difference between the left-hand side and the right?

In groups, choose one of these ideas and make up your own word-picture: a traffic-roundabout, a tower-block, a motorway (see the poem Motorways *for ideas), a football stadium, a railway station, a waterfall.*

Choose the best in each group, then exchange between groups.

For further examples, see Robert Froman's *Seeing Things*.

Weekend in the Country

Robert Froman

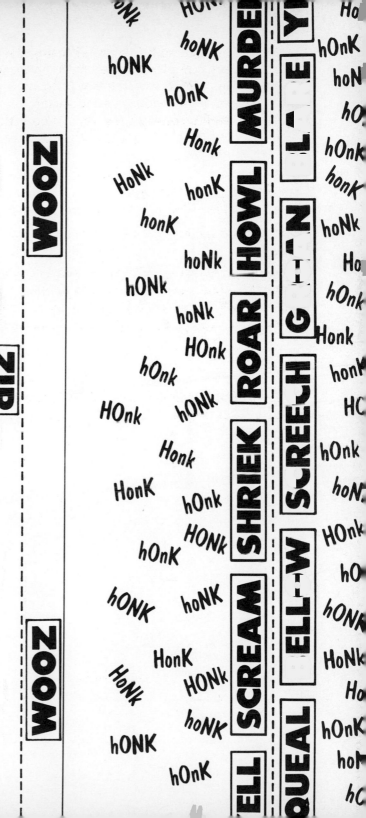

BRIDGE
FROM HERE TO THERE.

A FROZEN LEAP ACROSS THE WATER

Robert Froman

12

Bridge is a development of the idea on the previous page. It uses a whole phrase rather than single words in a **pattern** and also conveys a whole idea, even a new idea about a bridge, i.e. 'A frozen leap across the water'.

What do you think is meant by 'A frozen leap across the water'?

The words have been formed into the shape of a bridge; look at The Computer's First Christmas Card (page 77), *which has been set like a computer print-out.*

In groups choose one of the following ideas, make up a phrase including that idea (like Bridge *— from here to there), and then build words into a shape that fits the word:*

    a post-box, a dust-bin, a grandfather clock, a T.V., a telegraph pole, a bee-hive.

Now exchange the designs, discuss them and choose the best to be displayed.

Sky Day Dream goes on to express in its **pattern** not just a statement but a wish and a feeling; and to that extent it is closer to more usual poetry. By this stage the class will be well into the idea of playing with word-shapes. This is the most sophisticated application of it.

Why are the words in this shape?

Why do you think the poet wished to fly off with the crows?

Which of the three 'picture-poems' do you like most?

In groups, take one of the following ideas, write a sentence including the idea and further thoughts as well (just as this one includes crows flying and the poet's wish to join them), and build the whole sentence into a shape or design:

> *a grave-yard, a class-room, a housing estate, a boy's/girl's head, any other ideas you may have.*

Look for further poems, in *Junior Voices* particularly, where you think the shape has affected the poem in any way. A sense of shape and pattern in poetry is going to be increasingly important as the class progresses.

Examples:

> *French Persian Cats having a Ball JV* III:15
> *Orgy JV* III:23.

Sky Day Dream

WITH THEM

COULD FLY OFF

I WISHED THAT I

INTO THE SKY

FLY OFF

SOME CROWS

ONCE I SAW

Robert Froman

ladies and Jellyspoons,
i stand upon this speech to make a platforM,
the train I arrived in has not yet comE,
so I took a bus and walkeD.
i come before you to stand behind yoU
and tell you somethinG
i know nothing abouT.

one fine day in the middle of the nighT,
two dead men got up to fighT,
back to back they faced each otheR,
drew their swords and shot each otheR.
a paralysed donkey passing bY
kicked a blind man in the eyE,
knocked him through a nine inch wall,
into a dry ditch and drowned them all.

Playing with words and twisting them round for riddles, etc. can also be done with contradictions and opposites with much enjoyment: this involves manipulating a given **pattern**. *Ladles and Jellyspoons* is reminiscent of the Army message 'Send reinforcements, we're going to advance' finally arriving as 'Send three and fourpence, we're going to a dance.'

Here *Ladles and Jellyspoons* deals with confusion and contradictions, while *One fine day* deals with opposites and impossibilities. Ask some pupils to read these verses out to the class.

Read through these two verses again.

How many contradictions can you find in Ladles and Jellyspoons?

How many contradictions and opposites can you find in One fine day?

Do you know any different versions of these verses? or any other verses which include opposites like these?

Make up a verse or story of your own starting 'One snowy day in summer . . .'

For another version of *Ladles and Jellyspoons*, see *JV* III:76.
For another version of *One fine day* see *JV* II:8.
For further nonsense combinations, see
    Pete's Sweets *JV* I:6
    The Frog *JV* III:14.
For approaching things in the wrong order, see:
    The Story of a Story *JV* III:76
    After Ever Happily p. 65.

Don't forget the bacon is a modern version of 'Send reinforcements'. Although it was written as a children's story picture-book, its strong **pattern** and word-play with rhymes make it a poem. It is worth having a copy of the paperback (Picture Puffin) in the classroom. A child is sent to do some shopping and keeps saying over the list in his head. Unfortunately he sees things on his way that make him ask for the wrong items in the shop. The effort of remembering what he was told to get makes him forget the bacon.

How would you read this to get the maximum enjoyment out of it?

Make up your own shopping list of three items like 'Six farm eggs'.

Now change each item twice. 'Six farm eggs' becomes first 'Six fat legs' (seen at a bus stop) and then 'Six clothes pegs' (seen in a garden). Each set must rhyme, and should be of things you might see on the way to the shops.

You can draw pictures to decorate your lists.

This exercise quickly shows those who have difficulty with rhyme. If this goes well you could use Pat Hutchins's *The Surprise Party* in a similar way (also a Puffin). A development of this is Rhyming Slang. See especially: *JV* IV:94, 95 and *Jive Talk* in *JV* IV:41. See also *Names of Months JV* IV:7.

Don't Forget the Bacon!

Six farm eggs, a cake for tea, a pound of pears,
and don't forget the bacon.

Six fat legs, a cake for tea, a pound of pears
and don't forget the bacon.
Six fat legs, a cape for me, a pound of pears
and don't forget the bacon.
Six fat legs, a cape for me, a flight of stairs
and don't forget the bacon.
Six clothes pegs, a cape for me, a flight of stairs
and don't forget the bacon.
Six clothes pegs, a rake for leaves, a flight of stairs
and don't forget the bacon.
Six clothes pegs, a rake for leaves, a pile of chairs
and don't forget the bacon.

Six clothes pegs, a rake for leaves, and a pile of chairs, please.

A pile of chairs? A flight of stairs? – A POUND OF PEARS!
A rake for leaves? A cape for me? – A CAKE FOR TEA!
Six clothes pegs? Six fat legs? – SIX FARM EGGS!

*   *   *   *   *

Six farm eggs, a cake for tea, and a pound of pears

I FORGOT THE BACON

Pat Hutchins

15

I'm just going out for a moment
Why?

To make a cup of tea.
Why?

Because I'm thirsty.
Why?

Because it's hot.
Why?

Because the sun's shining.
Why?

Because it's summer.
Why?

Because that's when it is.
Why?

Why don't you stop saying why?
Why?

Tea-time why.
High-time-you-stopped-saying-why time.
What?

Michael Rosen

Conversations have a ready-made **pattern** to them and so often take on the form of a poem.

Building to a climax is another feature of pattern and form: the effect of this poem is that the questions are believable and the end is unexpected and amusing.

Ask the class to read the poem to themselves. Then choose two pupils to read it out as a conversation.

Who are the two people having this conversation?

Do you find this poem funny? If so, what is it that makes it funny?

What is special about the end of the poem?

For further conversation poems, see:

Which? JV II:29

Social Studies JV II:31

Get off this Estate JV IV:43.

Also compare this with other Michael Rosen poems in this book and in *Mind Your Own Business*. Show the class how he uses pattern, even if it is not always obvious (see especially 5,4,3,2,1 ... in *Mind Your own Business*).

Discuss where the pattern in some of his poems lies.

This poem may obviously be compared with the Rosen 'conversation' opposite. There is the same **pattern** and regularity to this conversation, but it also rhymes. The climax is a play on words, similar to the early jokes in this book. Ask the class to read the poem to themselves. Then choose two pupils to read it out as a conversation.

There is regular rhyming here: where is it?
What makes the ending special in this poem? Do you think it is good?
Which of these two 'conversation poems' do you prefer and why?

Compare other poems by Kit Wright in *Rabbiting On*. Point out how he uses pattern and rhyme. Perhaps he goes one step further than Rosen in pattern and form.

For longer conversation poems, see also:
    What's the Matter up There? JV II:33
    The Signifying Monkey JV II:39
    The Argument between Fin and Harpkin JV III:34.

Rabbiting On

Where did you go?
Oh . . . nowhere much.

What did you see?
Oh . . . rabbits and such.

Rabbits? What else?
Oh . . . a rabbit hutch.

What sort of rabbits?
What sort? Oh . . . small.

What sort of hutch?
Just a hutch, that's all.

But what did it look like?
Like a rabbit hutch.

Well, what was in it?
Small rabbits and such.

I worried about you
While you were gone.

*Why don't you stop
Rabbiting on?*

Kit Wright

twould be nice to be
an apostrophe
floating
above an s
hovering
like a paper kite
in between the its
eavesdropping, tiptoeing
high above the thats
an inky comet
spiralling
the highest tossed
of hats

Roger McGough

The third element of a poem that we can take out and consider is its **imagery** (see Introduction, page D). The poems on pages 18–26 can be used to develop an awareness of imagery of different kinds.

This first poem shows how one thing can be described in terms of another.

['Eavesdropping': originally eavesdrip was the water that dripped off the eaves or edge of a roof, and the eavesdrop was the area of ground that was likely to be dripped on. Thus an eaves-dropper was a person who stood within the eavesdrop to listen to secrets. He then became anyone who listened to private conversation. (*Oxford English Dictionary*)]

How many different things is the apostrophe like?
(kite, eavesdropper, tiptoe-er, comet, spiral, tossed-up hat)

[Explain the derivation of eavesdropper.]
Does the poem bring this word back to life? Does it help you get a picture of a secret listener?

Is it muddling to compare the apostrophe to so many different things?

Which comparison do you like best?

Write a similar poem about a question mark or a full stop.

See also the word-shapes on p. 10.

End of a Girl's First Tooth gives a very clear aural **image** in the word 'crithsps'. The little girl's speech is brought to life for us. We can also discuss whether or not it also creates a tactile image.

   Ice-Cream Poem continues the theme. It tells a simple story and uses images in a less obtrusive way. It provides a link with jokes and word-play. You might wish to discuss the appropriateness of the comparison with Lot's wife. What connection is there between a pillar of salt and whatever Ethel became?

You have five senses: sight, touch, hearing, smell, taste. Which of them does this poem rely on most?

Are any of the other four senses important in the poem?

What words can you collect that give the sound of things (e.g. buzz)?

How do you describe the noise of the ice-cream van's chimes?

Do you like yours better than 'booming tinkle'?

Do you think 'twinkle' is put in just for the rhyme or does it give you any kind of picture?

Could the word 'thaw' in verse 4 be muddling?

A similar word-play to *Ice-Cream Poem* is *Papa Moses Killed a Skunk* in *JV* I:8.

For other tall stories:
   How? So! *JV* III:53
   The Hobnailed Boots What Farver Wore *JV* IV:27
   and two tall stories *JV* IV:30.
And see also:
   The Big Rock Candy Mountains *NDBV*:112
   Jim Who Ran Away from his Nurse *NDBV*:109.

End of a Girl's First Tooth

Once she'd a tooth that wiggled;
Now she's a gap that lisps.
For weeks she could only suck lollies;
Now she champs peanuts and crithsps.

Roy Fuller

Ice-cream Poem

The chiefest of young Ethel's vices
Was eating multitudes of ices.

Whene'er the ice-van's booming tinkle
Was heard, Eth ran out in a twinkle,

And gorged herself on large 'Vanilla';
Her Mum foretold that it would kill 'er.

No tears could thaw her; once she ran
Away, and hid inside the van,

And promptly froze upon the spot
Like the saltpillar wife of Lot.

Poor Eth is licked! Behold the follies
Of one whose lolly went on lollies.

Gerda Mayer

19

Down at the Swimming Pool

Down at the swimming pool,
Kenny did a frog's hop,
Dave did a double dive,
And Peter did a belly-flop.

Bob sat in his bath at home,
Soaping sponge and flannel.
Said: *I'm working up towards
Swimming the English Channel.*

Gerda Mayer

Wink

I took 40 winks
yesterday afternoon
and another 40 today.
In fact I get through
about 280 winks a week.
Which is about 14,560
winks a year.
(The way I'm going on
I'll end up looking like a wink)

Roger McGough

Wink. This could be an opportunity to read the James Thurber story: *The Secret Life of James Thurber.* In this he describes how, as a child, he took expressions literally: she was crying her eyes out, he left town under a cloud, it's a simple lock – a skeleton will let you in. What makes this a poem?

What would a wink look like?
Is his arithmetic right?

See also:
   Boo Hoo JV I:9
   The Fence JV III:93
   The Yawn of Yawns JV III:57.

Down at the Swimming Pool
What picture of Bob do we get compared with Kenny, Dave, and Peter?
Why is the detail of 'soaping' important?
Do you find this a funny poem?

The obvious poem to read after this is *I had a Little Brother JV* I:8.

These two short and simple poems can be used to introduce the idea that words can give us a picture or an idea of a person.

What sort of girl is Rose? [Different answers should emerge. Discuss them.]

What sort of woman is the Duchess? Could she be right about her little boy?

Do those two four-line poems give us a picture of the people?

This is a place where you could introduce *Hard Cheese JV* III:68, and talk about the different **images** and characterizations in it. Or you could just enjoy it.

Duchess's Song

Speak roughly to your little boy,
    And beat him when he sneezes:
He only does it to annoy,
    Because he knows it teases.

Lewis Carroll

I am Rose

I am Rose my eyes are blue
I am Rose and who are you?
I am Rose and when I sing
I am Rose like anything.

Gertrude Stein

You can tell how wound up I am:
I can't even say 'Oh, damn!'
Just stutter, and point all round
With a slightly trembling hand.

Roy Fuller

'Full, over-full is my heart:
 Please take me away.'
'We'll send a dirty cart
 Every week. OK?'

Roy Fuller

Riddles are a good way of looking at **imagery**. 'Riddles are the only serious questions. Asking riddles is the only way you can make people aware of all you might mean. Riddles put all the possible answers into people's minds. They make people wonder . . .' *The Burr Wood* by Philip Glazebrook.

Points to look for: the accuracy of the description, and the ambiguity of words.

Answers: clock or watch
        dustbin.

Both these riddles are fairly simple. What gave away the answer?

What else did you think of?

What words misled you, even if only for a moment?

The next riddle is a version of a riddle of the Sphinx: What goes on 4 legs in the morning, 2 legs in the afternoon and 3 legs in the evening? (Answer: man as a baby, an adult, an old man with stick.) The poem is titled *Tree Gowns*. The title has been left out of the anthology. Its **imagery** is strong.

What is this?

What helped you to get the answer OR what made it difficult to find the answer?

Do you think it is helpful to compare the seasons with times of the day, or is it just confusing?

The second riddle is titled *AEIOU*. It depends on the ambiguity of 'in'. This can also be linked backwards to the word-shapes.

Can you guess what these 'little creatures' are?

Make up your own riddle based on the shapes of some letters.

Other riddles:
    JV II:1, III:2
    Love on the Canal Boat JV IV:76;
and the half-riddle *Shadows JV* I:12.

In the morning her dress is of palest green,
And in dark green in the heat of noon is she seen.
At evening she puts on a dress of rich gold,
But at night this poor lady is bare and cold.

James Reeves

Wind in March:
No leaves left
For its stiff summons.

We are very little creatures,
All of different voice and features;
One of us in *glass* is set,
One of us you'll find in *jet*.
T'other you may see in *tin*,
And the fourth a *box* within.
If the fifth you should pursue,
It can never fly from *you*.

Jonathan Swift

Too dense to have a door,
Window or fireplace or a floor,
They saw this cottage up,
Huge bricks of grass, clover and buttercup
Carting to byre and stable,
Where cow and horse will eat wall, roof and gable.

Andrew Young

Hard and black is my home,
Hard as a rock and black as night.
Scarlet and gold am I,
Delicate, warm and bright.

For long years I lie,
A prisoner in the dark,
Till at last I break my fetters
In a rush of flame and spark.

First tree and then a rock
The house where I sleep.
Now like a demon
I crackle and hiss and leap.

James Reeves

In our study of **imagery** we now move on from riddles to poems. Both of the poems on this page have been printed without their titles to show how like a riddle a short, descriptive poem is. The first is titled *The Haystack* and the second, *Fire*.

In what way is the first poem like a riddle?

Can you work out what it is describing?

Which group of words gave you the clue?

What is the second poem about?

What kind of fire is it?

What group gives you the best picture of what a coal fire looks like, sounds like, and feels like?

Write a poem about another kind of fire.

Similar poems that can be used to follow-up this page:

> *The House-Wreckers JV III:71*
> *An Ordinary Day JV IV:3*
> *Thunder and Lightning JV III:96*
> *Living Tenderly JV II:57*
> *Running Lightly over Spongy Ground JV III:66.*

Tom Bone is a development from the last few poems, but is a big step forward too. It starts almost like a riddle. Many children may miss the **imagery** altogether, especially on a superficial reading.

Who is Tom Bone?

Where exactly does he live?

What group of words first told you where he lives?

Which group of words in the first two verses gives you the best picture of the grave?

How would you read this poem? Practise and perform it.

The obvious poem to read after this is the same poet's *By St Thomas Water NDBV*:95.
See also
    Old Roger is Dead and Laid in his Grave JV I:23.
    And *Cowboy Song* on page 60 could be used to develop the theme.

TOM BONE

My name is Tom Bone,
I live all alone
In a deep house on Winter Street.
　　Through my mud wall
　　The wolf-spiders crawl
　　And the mole has his beat.

On my roof of green grass
All the day footsteps pass
In the heat and the cold,
　　As snug in a bed
　　With my name at its head
　　One great secret I hold.

Tom Bone, when the owls rise
In the drifting night skies
Do you walk round about?
　　All the solemn hours through
　　I lie down just like you
　　And sleep the night out.

Tom Bone, as you lie there
On your pillow of hair,
What grave thoughts do you keep?
　　Tom says, 'Nonsense and stuff!
　　You'll know soon enough.
　　Sleep, darling, sleep.'

Charles Causley

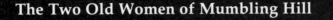

The Two Old Women of Mumbling Hill

The two old trees on Mumbling Hill,
They whisper and chatter and never keep still.
What do they say as they lean together
In rain or sunshine or windy weather?

There were two women lived near the hill,
And they used to gossip as women will
Of friends and neighbours, houses and shops,
Weather and trouble and clothes and crops.

And one sad winter they both took ill,
The two old women of Mumbling Hill.
They were bent and feeble and wasted away
And both of them died on the selfsame day.

Now the ghosts of the women of Mumbling Hill,
They started to call out loud and shrill,
'Where are the tales we used to tell,
And where is the talking we loved so well?'

In this poem the picture of two old trees that look like old women has led to the story that the poem tells. The **visual image** and the **aural image** must both be strongly conveyed by the words of the poem if it is to succeed.

Do you get a clear picture of the trees just from the first four lines?
Do you like the idea of the ghosts taking root and turning into trees?
Which group of words gives you the clearest picture of the trees?
How would you arrange a reading of the poem?

For a development of the taking root idea, see:
  Tree-Disease JV II:29.
See also:
  The Two Roots JV II:67
  Natural Song JV III:28.

Side by side stood the ghosts until
They both took root on Mumbling Hill;
And they turned to trees, and they slowly grew,
Summer and winter the long years through.

In the winter the bare boughs creaked and cried,
In summer the green leaves whispered and sighed,
And still they talk of fine and rain,
Storm and sunshine, comfort and pain.

The two old trees of Mumbling Hill,
They whisper and chatter and never keep still.
What do they say as they lean together
In rain or sunshine or windy weather?

Small, Smaller

I thought that I knew all there was to know
Of being small, until I saw once, black against the snow,
A shrew, trapped in my footprint, jump and fall
And jump again and fall, the hole too deep, the walls too
   tall.

Russell Hoban

The Fly

How large unto the tiny fly
   Must little things appear!—
A rosebud like a feather bed,
   Its prickle like a spear;

A dewdrop like a looking-glass,
   A hair like golden wire;
The smallest grain of mustard-seed
   As fierce as coals of fire;

A loaf of bread, a lofty hill,
   A wasp, a cruel leopard;
And specks of salt as bright to see
   As lambskins to a shepherd.

Walter de la Mare

Small, Smaller is a poem about **feelings**, describing a very small incident and evoking sympathy for an animal. The size of the animals is conveyed very vividly, as it is also with *The Fly*. Imagery is used to convey the size: the imagery of 'walls' in the first poem, 'spear', 'coals', etc. in the second.

What exactly did the poet see in Small, Smaller?

How do we know that the poet himself felt small at the time?

How is the shrew shown to be very small?

In The Fly *what things in a fly's life are compared with things in a human's life?*

Why would each of these things appear to the fly as they are described?

Why would 'the smallest grain of mustard-seed' be 'as fierce as coals of fire'?

Can you think of any other objects a fly might meet and what 'human' objects they might be compared with?

For further comparisons of animal life with human, see *NDBV* for *Fishes' Heaven, The Snail, Gorilla*; and compare *A Children's Zoo* (Armada Lion).
Also:
>   *Indomitable JV* III:19
>   *Interruption to a Journey JV* IV:6.

Sympathy for small creatures on p. 28 is contrasted here with lack of **feeling** for similar creatures. These two poems are about the abuse of animals as pets or entertainers, and should strike a chord with children. *Bells of Heaven* can lead to discussions about circuses, while *Take One Home* considers the drawbacks of keeping pets.

What would 'ring the bells of heaven'?

What is meant by lines 3–4?

Why are the tigers likely to be 'shabby'?

Four different situations of humans using animals are referred to here: what are they?

In Take One Home *what is being described in the first verse?* [A 'dam' is a mother.]

The creature is being kept in very poor conditions: how many details of these conditions are mentioned?

What exactly is meant by lines 5–6?

What sort of animal is being talked about here?

Have you ever had an experience like this with a pet? Perhaps you found the novelty wore off or it died of neglect? It usually happens to smaller animals, such as fish, hamsters, gerbils.

Compare:
    Auguries of Innocence NDBV:58
    The Snare NDBV:84
    Upstairs JV III:20
    The Meadow Mouse JV IV:15.

The Bells of Heaven

'Twould ring the bells of Heaven
The wildest peal for years,
If Parson lost his senses
And people came to theirs,
And he and they together
Knelt down with angry prayers
For tamed and shabby tigers
And dancing dogs and bears,
And wretched, blind pit ponies,
And little hunted hares.

Ralph Hodgson

Take One Home for the Kiddies

On shallow straw, in shadeless glass,
Huddled by empty bowls, they sleep:
No dark, no dam, no earth, no grass –
Mam, get us one of them to keep.

Living toys are something novel,
But it soon wears off somehow.
Fetch the shoebox, fetch the shovel –
Mam, we're playing funerals now.

Philip Larkin

*Wasp in May
Storing his venom
For a long summer.*

In the daytime I am Rob Roy and a tiger
In the daytime I am Marco Polo
          I chase bears in Bricket Wood
In the daytime I am the Tower of London
          nothing gets past me
          when it's my turn
          in Harrybo's hedge
In the daytime I am Henry the fifth and Ulysses
          and I tell stories
          that go on for a whole week
          if I want.
     At night in the dark
          when I've shut the front room door
          I try and
          get up the stairs across the landing
          into bed and under the pillow
          without breathing once.

     Michael Rosen

          The Dark

          I feared the darkness as a boy;
          And if at night I had to go
          Upstairs alone I'd make a show
          Of carrying on with those below
          A dialogue of shouts and 'whats?'
          So they'd be sure to save poor Roy
          Were he attacked by vampire bats.

          Or thugs or ghosts. But far less crude
          Than criminal or even ghost
          Behind a curtain or a post
          Was what I used to dread the most –
          The always-unseen bugaboo
          Of black-surrounded solitude.
          I dread it still at sixty-two.

          Roy Fuller

The next few poems (pp. 30–35) deal with fear of the dark and of loneliness in the dark, a familiar **feeling** to most children even if some will not admit it. They suggest the 'unknown' of night-time and the tricks the imagination can play.

The Rob Roy poem compares the self-confidence of day-time with the panic of night. Ask the class to read this to themselves and then ask one pupil to read it out.

Who were Rob Roy and Marco Polo?

What is happening in Harrybo's hedge?

Why should he tell stories 'that go on for a whole week'?

In what way do all the boasts in the daytime show he is confident and happy?

How does Michael Rosen show the speed with which he travels in the dark at night?

Why 'without breathing once'?

What do you fear about the dark in your house?

For feelings in the dark, compare *The Dark* on the opposite page, and *The Man who Wasn't There* on the next page.

For pattern, compare Rosen's *Father says*, and *My Dad's Thumb*. There is a pattern in *Rob Roy* – each 'daytime' line contains a new idea – but speed and panic are conveyed in the later lines by combining ideas.

This poem on The Dark by a different poet mentions specific things in the dark which are frightening to the imagination, and has a more solemn reflection at the end from the grown man.

[cont

What did he do as he went upstairs alone to bed?

What different things are mentioned that he was afraid of?

What do you think is 'black-surrounded solitude'?

Why should he dread it still at sixty-two?

Read the poem to yourselves. Now who would like to read it out to the class, making the frightening things sound frightening?

Compare: *The Man who Wasn't there* (p. 33), and perhaps:
> *Acquainted with the night* NDBV:229
> *The Listeners* NDBV:209.

Also:
> *The Witch! The Witch!* JV I:18
> *Be a Monster* p. 52.

Carrying on from *The Dark* this poem is a story about fear of the dark and the unknown, and the wild workings of the imagination. Ask the class to read it to themselves, then read out the refrain together, with three pupils reading a verse each.

Who is 'the man' or what is he?

Why is the 'shadow-coat' 'shapeless' and 'hanging about'?
('hanging about' has two meanings here)

What is 'broken light', and why is the black suit 'shaking'?

How could he 'swim across the floor'?

What exactly is the last verse describing?

Read the poem aloud [as described above].

Refer back to *The Dark* and also to *Hist Wist*.
The Listeners NDBV:29 and *The Trap* NDBV:210 are examples of the imagination creating frightening things.
See also:
   The Way to the Boiler was Dark JV III:71
   I Know some Lonely Houses JV III:73.

The Man who Wasn't There

Yesterday upon the stair
I met a man who wasn't there;
He wasn't there again today,
I wish, I wish, he'd go away.

I've seen his shapeless shadow-coat
Beneath the stairway, hanging about;
And outside, muffled in a cloak
The same colour as the dark;

I've seen him in a black, black suit
Shaking, under the broken light;
I've seen him swim across the floor
And disappear beneath the door;

And once, I almost heard his breath
Behind me, running up the path:
Inside, he leant against the wall,
And turned .. and was no one at all.

Yesterday upon the stair
I met a man who wasn't there;
He wasn't there again today,
I wish, I wish, he'd go away.

Brian Lee

Goodbat Nightman

God bless all policemen
and fighters of crime,
May thieves go to jail
for a very long time.

They've had a hard day
helping clean up the town,
Now they hang from the mantelpiece
both upside down.

A glass of warm blood
and then straight up the stairs,
Batman and Robin
are saying their prayers.

They've locked all the doors
and they've put out the bat,
Put on their batjamas
(They like doing that)

They've filled their batwater-bottles
made their batbeds,
With two springy battresses
for sleepy batheads.

They're closing red eyes
and they're counting black sheep,
Batman and Robin
are falling asleep.

Roger McGough

The image of Batman combining man and bat, and being on the side of 'good' has captured children's imaginations. Spiderman is another example of this imagery.

This poem does many things: it makes these mysterious creatures attractive, it plays with words, it combines the tone of bed-time prayers with that of a story. Compared with the preceding poems, it makes horrific night-time **feelings** bearable, amusing, and even comfortable.

Why should they hang upside-down from the mantelpiece?

What usual bed-time activities are mentioned in the poem, but altered for Batman and Robin?

Are there any features of the poem that are frightening?

Why do you think Batman is a popular character?

Compare *The Bat*, opposite, for a more realistic view.

It is but a small jump from Batman back to a real bat, with reference to its human features and its genuinely frightening characteristics. This poem starts by describing the creature vividly, then finishes on an ominous note of mystery, evoking **feelings** of fear and bewilderment.

In what way is the bat 'cousin to the mouse' in day-time?
How do his fingers 'make a hat about his head'?
What exactly is being described in verse 3?
What is frightening about brushing against a screen?
What is it that makes bats frightening? There are several different features, if you think about it.

Compare *Be a Monster, Hairy Toe, Horrible Things* for alarming ideas. Compare *Horrible Song* for another alarming flying creature (the crow) (pp. 52, 54, 70).
See *Hist Whist*.

The Bat

By day the bat is cousin to the mouse.
He likes the attic of an ageing house.

His fingers make a hat about his head.
His pulse is so slow we think him dead.

He loops in crazy figures half the night
Among the trees that face the corner light.

But when he brushes up against a screen,
We are afraid of what our eyes have seen:

For something is amiss or out of place
When mice with wings can wear a human face.

Theodore Roethke

The dinosaurs are not all dead.
I saw one raise its iron head
To watch me walking down the road
Beyond our house today.
Its jaws were dripping with a load
Of earth and grass that it had cropped.
It must have heard me where I stopped,
Snorted white steam my way,
And stretched its long neck out to see,
And chewed, and grinned quite amiably.

Charles Malam

36

We return to our study of **image** with a group of poems on streets and street creatures. The first is almost a riddle. Its title is *Steam shovel*; in England the machine would probably be called a digger.

What is being described?

In what ways is the digger like a dinosaur?

('Its jaws were dripping . . .') What would you expect a dinosaur's jaws to be dripping with?

What other group of words or word gives you a picture of the digger?

Do you get any sound pictures of the machine?

Similar poems are:
> *The Chant of the Awakening Bulldozers*
> and *To A Giraffe* JV I:44, 45
> *The Garden Hose* JV III:22
> *The Toaster* JV III:7
> *About an Excavation* JV III:44.

This poem combines aural and visual **imagery**. In places we could criticize its accuracy of observation but the overall effect remains strong. It is important that the point of the poem is understood. We are not on the motorway itself but looking up at an elevated stretch of urban road on stilts.

What sound pictures do you get of the motorway?

What sight pictures do you get?

In what way does the motorway dwarf *us? Do you think that this is still a living comparison? Does it make you think of dwarfs, or just of it being big?*

Do you think that the cars look like fleas?

Is there anything wrong with the joining of 'fleas' and 'fly by'?

What makes the stamping sound?

How would you read this poem?

Particularly relevant here is *Gravel Paths* JV II:32.

Motorway

Motorway – motorway – motorway,
Never stay – never stay – never stay,
Broad bridge ribbon overrides us,
Giant-strides us,
Manmade dinosaurus, dwarfs us.

Motor-metal fleas fly by,
Whining car horns grow and die,
Skim the giant's broad black back,
White line,
Sign post,
Motor track.

Listen in your sleep, dream deep,
Hear him stamp his giant feet,
Beating, beating, street on street,
Motorway – motorway – motorway.

Marian Lines

With *It's a Lean Car* we have **images** to create an idea, in this case that of speed. *Carbreakers* seems to come alive only in the last verse. What does your class think?

What did the first line of the poem make you think was going to come next?

When you think of old car bodies do you think of 'steel and paint and tin'?

What pictures does this poem give you?

Is there any sound that she might really hear at night?

What picture of the lean car do you get?

Which of the two comparisons do you prefer?

Other poems:
> *The Government Said* etc. JV III:47 to 49
> *The Legs* JV III:61
> *Southbound on the Freeway* JV IV:54
> *A Dream of Metals* JV IV:60
> *The Great Figure* JV I:2
> *The Squad Car* JV I:33.

Carbreakers

There's a graveyard in our street
But it's not for putting people in;
The bodies that they bury here
Are made of steel and paint and tin.

The people come and leave their wrecks
For crunching in the giant jaws
Of a great hungry car machine,
That lives on bonnets, wheels and doors.

When I pass by the yard at night,
I sometimes think I hear a sound
Of ghostly horns that moan and whine,
Upon that metal graveyard mound.

Marian Lines

It's a Lean Car

It's a lean car . . . a long legged dog of a car
    a grey ghost eagle car.
The feet of it eat the dirt of a road . . . the wings of it
    eat the hills.

Carl Sandburg

February evening:
A cold puddle of petrol
Makes its own rainbow.

Sea-wash

The sea-wash never ends.
The sea-wash repeats, repeats.
Only old songs? Is that all the sea knows?
        Only the old strong songs?
        Is that all?
The sea-wash repeats, repeats.

Carl Sandburg

The Tide in the River

The tide in the river,
The tide in the river,
The tide in the river runs deep,
    I saw a shiver
    Pass over the river
As the tide turned in its sleep.

Eleanor Farjeon

Moved

The great sea stirs me.
The great sea sets me adrift,
it sways me like the weed
on a river-stone.

The sky's height stirs me.
The strong wind blows through my mind.
It carries me with it,
so I shake with joy.

Uvavnuk

In contrast to the previous group here is a set of beach poems in which the **pattern** does much to create the images, which in turn should stir feelings. The poems must be read aloud to bring out the rhythm and the value of repetition. It is best to present them together.

Which of the four poems gives you the best feeling for the movement of the sea?

How does it work?

Which has the best sound pictures? Is it the same as your choice for the best picture of movement?

A Beach of Stones is a more difficult poem concerned with the sound of pebbles on the beach. It will need discussion to bring out the meaning.

What picture does 'stadium' give? Does 'roaring' help this?

How does water strike at the stones?

What happens to them?

Which of these sea poems do you like best?

How would you arrange them, and say them, for a reading?

See also:
  A Conversation JV II:5
  The New River JV IV:50
  The section *Seascapes* in *NDBV*
  The Puffin Book of Salt-Sea Verse.

Beach of Stones

That stadium of roaring stones,
The suffering. O they are not dumb things,
Though bleached and worn, when water
Strikes at them. Stones will be the last ones;
They are earth's bones, no easy prey
For breakers. And they are not broken
But diminish only, under the pestle,
Under protest. They shift through centuries,
Grinding their way towards silence.

Kevin Crossley-Holland

Morning in June:
On the sea's horizon
A white island, alone.

Washing-up Song

Chip the glasses and crack the plates!
　　Blunt the knives and bend the forks!
That's what Bilbo Baggins hates –
　　Smash the bottles and burn the corks!

Cut the cloth and tread on the fat!
　　Pour the milk on the pantry floor!
Leave the bones on the bedroom mat!
　　Splash the wine on every door!

Dump the crocks in a boiling bowl;
　　Pound them up with a thumping pole;
And when you've finished, if any are whole,
Send them down the hall to roll!

That's what Bilbo Baggins hates!
So, carefully! carefully with the plates!

J. R. R. Tolkien

Sink Song

Scouring out the porridge pot,
　　Round and round and round!

Out with all the scraith and scoopery,
Lift the eely ooly droopery,
Chase the glubbery slubbery gloopery
　　Round and round and round!

Out with all the doleful dithery,
　　Ladle out the slimy slithery,
Hunt and catch the hithery thithery,
　　Round and round and round!

Out with all the obbly gubbly,
On the stove it burns so bubbly,
Use the spoon and use it doubly,
　　Round and round and round!

J. A. Lindon

Playing with words involves the use of rhyme and other sounds for their own sake, combined in a **pattern**. The Bilbo song about washing-up creates the effect of noise by regular rhythm and rhyme, short words and several onomatopoeic effects. Read it out to the class, showing the beat clearly as four to a line (Chíp the glásses and cráck the plátes).

'Sink Song' goes further. Here playing with words extends to inventing words to convey certain sounds and consistencies.

Read the Bilbo Baggins song all together as a chant. Make sure there are four beats to a line.

Which of the words sound like the noise they describe? (For example, the word 'crack' sounds like the noise of something cracking. This effect is called 'onomatopoeia'.)

In this poem which words are particularly good to shout to show you are angry?

Read Sink Song *all together. There are again four beats to each line except 'Round and round and round' which has three.*

Pick out the made-up words from Sink-Song *and suggest what bits of mess in a sink of washing-up each might be describing.*

For attitudes to washing up, see:
    Accidentally JV III:37.
For invented words of anger, see:
    Mean Song JV II:43.
For 'sound' words, see:
    Words to be Said JV II:74–7, III:38–41, 56, IV:24, 26.
For playing with one sound, see:
    A Canner JV III:44.
For invented words in rhythm, see:
    A Computer's First Christmas Card p. 77.
For sound words and onomatopoeia, see:
    Cataract of Lodore on p. 44.

In *NO!* the poet plays with words in a different way, by repetition rather than invention. The **pattern** of the repeated sound 'no' together with the image conveyed by 'no' make for a depressing picture, added to the images of bleak, monotonous November in the rest of the poem. (Perhaps the teacher should read this poem to the class first, without them seeing it, for the first effect of the final point.)

How does the poet suggest that the light is the same all through the day in November?

How does he suggest that you cannot see very far?

How does he suggest people are not very friendly in November?

How does he suggest life is rather dull?

How does he suggest that you feel uncomfortable and depressed in yourself? (a 'member' is here a 'limb').

Do you think he exaggerates? If so, in which particular points?

For another treatment of this time of year see *November Story*, p. 74. Ideally these poems should be considered during the month of November, when the pupils can see the effects for themselves.

For more sound poems, see:
   J is for Jazz Man JV I:14
   House Moving JV I:41.

NO!

No sun – no moon!
No morn – no noon –
No dawn – no dusk – no proper time of day –
No sky – no earthly view –
No distance looking blue –
No road – no street – no 't'other side the way' –
No end to any Row –
No indications where the Crescents go –
No top to any steeple –
No recognitions of familiar people –
No courtesies for showing 'em –
No knowing 'em! –
No travelling at all – no locomotion,
No inkling of the way – no notion –
'No go' – by land or ocean –
No mail – no post –
No news from any foreign coast –
No Park – no Ring – no afternoon gentility –
No company – no nobility –
No warmth, no cheerfulness, no healthful ease,
No comfortable feel in any member –
No shade, no shine, no butterflies, no bees,
No fruits, no flowers, no leaves, no birds, –
November!

Thomas Hood

from The Cataract of Lodore

The Cataract strong
Then plunges along,
Striking and raging
As if a war waging
Its caverns and rocks among:
Rising and leaping,
Sinking and creeping,
Swelling and sweeping,
Showering and springing,
Flying and flinging,
Writhing and ringing,
Eddying and whisking,
Spouting and frisking,
Turning and twisting,
Around and around
With endless rebound!
Smiting and fighting,
A sight to delight in;
Confounding, astounding,
Dizzying and deafening the ear with its sound.

This extract from *The Cataract of Lodore*, is an extreme and effective example of playing with and inventing words to produce a **pattern** with a cumulative effect, conveying both sound and action.

(The whole poem may be found in the *Oxford Book of Children's Verse.*)

Read through the poem to yourselves.

Think about the different sights and sounds you might hear at or near a waterfall: now find words or pairs of words that bring out different sounds in the poem (e.g. 'sprinkling and twinkling', bring out a different sound from 'bubbling and troubling').

Are there any words here you think the poet had invented for the purpose? Use a dictionary to check your ideas.

Are there any words you think he has used wrongly or which you do not think are good?

You might think the poet could have made his effect without such a long list of words. Why do you think he went on for so long (and this is not the whole poem)?

Divide this piece up for reading by groups, then read it aloud in groups: let the words make their noises fully and keep the speed up – like a waterfall.

Experiment with words yourselves in a similar way, writing your own description of a railway station, a football stadium, fireworks or any other noisy scene that occurs to you.

Compare *She is far from the Land*, also by Thomas Hood, in *The Puffin Book of Salt Sea Verse* p. 111.

Dividing and gliding and sliding,
And falling and brawling and sprawling,
And driving and riving and striving,
And sprinkling and twinkling and wrinkling,
And sounding and bounding and rounding,
And bubbling and troubling and doubling,
And grumbling and rumbling and tumbling,
And clattering and battering and shattering;
Retreating and beating and meeting and sheeting,
Delaying and straying and playing and spraying,
Advancing and prancing and glancing and dancing,
Recoiling, turmoiling and toiling and boiling,
And gleaming and streaming and steaming and beaming,
And rushing and flushing and brushing and gushing,
And flapping and rapping and clapping and slapping,
And curling and whirling and purling and twirling,
And thumping and plumping and bumping and jumping,
And dashing and flashing and splashing and clashing;
And so never ending, but always descending,
Sounds and motions for ever and ever are blending,
All at once and all o'er, with a mighty uproar,
And this way the Water comes down at Lodore.

Robert Southey

My dad's thumb
can stick pins in wood
without flinching –
it can crush family-size matchboxes
in one stroke
and lever off jam-jar lids without piercing
at the pierce here sign.

If it wanted
it could be a bath-plug
or a paint-scraper
a keyhole cover or a tap-tightener.

It's already a great nutcracker
and if it dressed up
it could easily pass
as a broad bean or a big toe.

In actual fact, it's quite simply
the world's fastest envelope burster.

Michael Rosen

Father says
Never
let
me
see
you
doing
that
again
father says
tell you once
tell you a thousand times
come hell or high water
his finger drills my shoulder
never let me see you doing that again

My brother knows all his phrases off by heart
so we practise them in bed at night.

Michael Rosen

In *My dad's thumb* there is inventive use of **image** to describe a simple object like a thumb. The simple idea is given unusual twists: and in more sophisticated poetry ordinary things are observed from unusual angles. The poem begins to introduce the idea of metaphor, with the thumb being called a bath-plug, a tap-tightener, a nutcracker, and so on.

There is no regular pattern, but each line contains a new image. Remove the first line and it could be another riddle.

Which words show that Dad's thumb is special?

How many uses of a thumb are mentioned here?

In groups think of some more uses for a man's thumb.

In groups think about another object (e.g. a fork, a wellington boot) and list various uses, including some unlikely ones.

Write the uses out, putting each on a new line and leaving the most unexpected until last.

For similar use of images to describe ordinary objects.
See also:
> *It's a Lean Car* p. 39
> *The Tide in the River* p. 40
> *Steam Shovel* p. 36
> *Tree Gowns* p. 23.

In *Father says* the same poet uses **pattern** to build up to an anti-climax, whereas in the first poem the pattern builds to a climax. Again each line makes a point and shows how it should be read.

Read it out to the class, giving full value to the line division; and after discussion ask one or two of the pupils to read it out.

[cont

*Why is there one word per line in the first half (apart from the first line)?
Does it affect how it is read?*

*What is meant by 'come hell or high water'? Do you know other ways of
saying this?*

'His finger drills my shoulder'? What does this mean?

For more poems by Michael Rosen, showing his use of pattern and
his building to a climax, see his other books: *Mind Your Own
Business* and *Wouldn't You Like To Know*.

My Dad, your Dad is an extension of the earlier conversation poems
like *Why?* and *Rabbiting On*. It builds to a climax or pointed ending.
This retains the **pattern** of dialogue but adds rhythm and rhyme.

What in the poem makes one Dad 'thicker' than the other?

What makes one Dad more boring? How does the poet show he is boring?

Why might some people think this a strange way to talk about Dads?

How does each speaker show that he really admires his Dad?

*Read the poem through again carefully, then read it out in pairs. Each
member of the pair takes a verse, but remember to do alternate lines in the
last verse.*

Have you enjoyed this poem? If so, why do you think it was enjoyable?

For more exploits of Dad, see *Rabbiting On* by Kit Wright.
For a similar point of description, see *The Count Duke   JV* IV:45.
For further conversation poems, see *Conversation* (from *Under Milk
Wood*) *JV* II:5 and pages 4–5, 16–17, 52, 62 in this book.

My Dad, Your Dad

My dad's fatter than your dad,
Yes, my dad's fatter than yours:
If he eats any more he won't fit in the house,
He'll have to live out of doors.

Yes, but my dad's balder than your dad,
My dad's balder, O.K.,
He's only got two hairs left on his head
And both are turning grey.

Ah, but my dad's thicker than your dad,
My dad's thicker, all right.
He has to look at his watch to see
If it's noon or the middle of the night.

Yes, but my dad's more boring than your dad.
If he ever starts counting sheep
When he can't get to sleep at night, he finds
It's the sheep that go to sleep.

But my dad doesn't mind your dad.
Mine quite likes yours too.
I suppose they don't always think much of US!
That's true, I suppose, that's true.

Kit Wright

My Father

Some fathers work at the office, others work at the store,
Some operate great cranes and build up skyscrapers galore,
Some work in canning factories counting green peas into cans,
Some drive all night in huge and thundering removal vans.

But mine has the strangest job of the lot.
My Father's the Chief Inspector of –
    What?
O don't tell the mice, don't tell the moles,
My Father's the Chief Inspector of
    HOLES.

It's a work of the highest importance because you never know
What's in a hole, what fearful thing is creeping from below.
Perhaps it's a hole to the ocean and will soon gush water in tons,
Or maybe it leads to a vast cave full of gold and skeletons.

Though a hole might seem to have nothing but dirt in,
Somebody's simply got to make certain.
Caves in the mountain, clefts in the wall,
My Father has to inspect them all.

In *My dad's thumb* the poet considered a wide variety of uses for a thumb. In *My Father* the same is done for holes. Various **images** are conjured up from the simple idea of a hole. Again a simple idea is being considered from unusual angles, and this is carried to fantastic proportions.

The regular rhythm and rhyme often heighten the light-heartedness (e.g. 'dirt in'/'curtain'). Read it to the class, bringing out the rhythm.

How is Father's job made to seem more important than an Inspector of Holes sounds at first?

How many possible causes of holes are mentioned?

Try and find the beat in verses, 3, 5, 7. Then offer to read it out to a rhythm. How many beats are there to a line?

Now find the beat in verses 2, 4, 6, 8. How many beats to a line? Read it out, in groups, each group taking one verse.

For other Ted Hughes' relatives, see:
    Meet My Folks by Ted Hughes.
For other poems about characters, see:
    Mr Tom Narrow p. 50
    Zeke p. 51;
    and the *People* section in *NDBV*.

That crack in the road looks harmless. My Father knows it's not.
The world may be breaking into two and starting at that spot.
Or maybe the world is a great egg, and we live on the shell,
And it's just beginning to split and hatch: you simply cannot tell.

If you see a crack, run to the phone, run!
My Father will know just what's to be done.
A rumbling hole, a silent hole,
My Father will soon have it under control.

Keeping a check on all these holes he hurries from morning to night.
There might be sounds of marching in one, or an eye shining bright.
A tentacle came groping from a hole that belonged to a mouse,
A floor collapsed and Chinamen swarmed up into the house.

A Hole's an unpredictable thing –
Nobody knows what a Hole might bring.
Caves in the mountain, clefts in the wall,
My Father has to inspect them all!

Ted Hughes

Mr Tom Narrow

A scandalous man
　　Was Mr Tom Narrow,
He pushed his grandmother
　　Round in a barrow.
And he called out loud
　　As he rang his bell,
'Grannies to sell!
　　Old grannies to sell!'

The neighbours said,
　　As they passed them by,
'This poor old lady
　　We will not buy.
He surely must be
　　A mischievous man
To try for to sell
　　His own dear Gran.'

'Besides,' said another,
　　'If you ask me,
She'd be very small use
　　That I can see.'
'You're right,' said a third,
　　'And no mistake –
A very poor bargain
　　She'd surely make.'

So Mr Tom Narrow
　　He scratched his head,
And he sent his grandmother
　　Back to bed;
And he rang his bell
　　Through all the town
Till he sold his barrow
　　For half a crown.

James Reeves

Mr Tom Narrow is an example of a poem telling a **story.** It has a regular pattern and, like the preceding poems about Dad and Father, tells us features of the person and his character. It appeals because of the man's odd occupation. Is this a cruel poem?

Why do you think the poet calls the man Tom Narrow?
Why should he want to sell his Gran?
Why would she make 'a very poor bargain'?
Why did he sell his barrow instead?

For further poems about characters, see:

Zeke uses aural **imagery**. When you hear the poem read as it is spelt, you can imagine Zeke speaking and you can hear him with his stick tapping his way up the aisle.

   After reading it aloud to the class, it will be necessary to explain that 'crippin'' is 'creeping', 'haisle' is 'aisle'; and also explain what an aisle is, and what a ferrule on the end of a stick is.

What is meant by 'gnarly'? What else might it describe?

What different things does the poem tell you about Zeke?

What does the last line mean?

Ask one or two pupils to read the poem out, capturing the dialect indicated by the spelling.

For dialect affecting the reading of a poem, see *Beg parding JV* II:49.

Zeke

Gnarly and bent and deaf's a post
Pore ole Ezekiel Purvis
Goeth crippin' slowly up the 'ill
To the Commoonion Survis.

And tappy tappy up the haisle
Goeth stick and brassy ferrule:
And Passon 'ath to stoopy down
An' 'olley in ees yerole.

L. A. G. Strong

Horrible Things

'What's the horriblest thing you've seen?'
Said Nell to Jean.

'Some grey-coloured, trodden-on plasticine;
On a plate, a left-over cold baked bean;
A cloak-room ticket numbered thirteen;
A slice of meat without any lean;
The smile of a spiteful fairy-tale queen;
A thing in the sea like a brown submarine;
A cheese fur-coated in brilliant green;
A bluebottle perched on a piece of sardine.
What's the horriblest thing *you've* seen?'
Said Jean to Nell.

'Your face, as you tell
Of all the horriblest things you've seen.'

Roy Fuller

'Be a Monster'

I am a frightful monster,
My face is cabbage green
And even with my mouth shut
My teeth can still be seen.
My finger-nails are like rats' tails
And very far from clean.

I cannot speak a language
But make a wailing sound
It could be any corner
You find me coming round.
Then, arms outspread
And eyeballs red,
I skim across the ground.

The girls scream out and scatter
From this girl-eating bat.
I usually catch a small one
Because her legs are fat;
Or it may be she's tricked by me
Wearing her grandpa's hat.

Roy Fuller

The **image** of what is horrible is conveyed in this poem by random examples. Many of the items will arouse similar feelings in the class. There is also the additional effect of all the lines rhyming on a rather unpleasant sound '-een'/'-ean'. Make sure the reading brings this out.

Think about each of the horrible things mentioned, in turn, and say why you, or anyone else, might find them horrible.

As you have been talking about these things, have you noticed the effect the ideas have had on the faces of others in the class? What did they look like?

A lot of the ideas in the poem are about food; can you think of any others connected with food that you would feel strongly about?

What other examples can you think of 'the horriblest thing you've seen'?

For further horrible ideas, see:
> *Hairy Toe* p. 54
> *The Horrible Song* p. 70
> *Be Merry* JV III:32
> *The Trap* NDBV:210
> *Would You Rather?* by John Burningham (Cape).

[cont

In *Be a Monster* the effect is created by **images** of colour and sound, parts of the monster's body and other unpleasant creatures.

Read the poem to the class as 'horribly' as you can.

What colours are mentioned in the poem? Why are those colours particularly frightening or startling?

What noises are mentioned? Why are they frightening?

What parts of the body of the monster are mentioned? Why are these parts particularly alarming?

What unpleasant creatures are mentioned? Why are 'rat' and 'bat' frightening creatures? Why are 'rat' and 'bat' frightening words?

Read the poem aloud in groups, each group chanting one verse in a menacing way.

Draw and colour this monster.

Draw and colour a monster of your own. Then write a description of it, using colours, sounds, parts of its body – perhaps with some rhymes.

For further monsters and horrible creatures, see:

Oliphaunt JV II:49
The Magical Mouse JV II:61
Sonnet 72 JV III:75
In the Orchard JV IV:44.

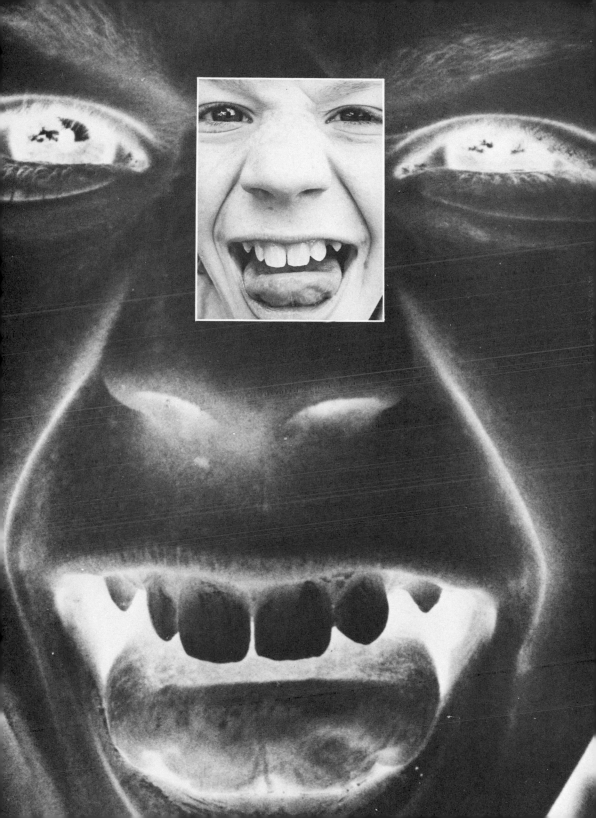

The Hairy Toe

Once there was a woman went out to pick beans,
and she found a Hairy Toe.
She took the Hairy Toe home with her,
and that night, when she went to bed,
the wind began to moan and groan.
Away off in the distance
she seemed to hear a voice crying,
'Where's my Hair-r-ry To-o-e?
Who's got my Hair-r-ry To-o-oe?'

This well-known poem contains further **images** of nastiness and of what is horrible. It can be quite frightening, read with full value given to the onomatopoeia, the sinister repetition, and with increased volume towards the end of the verse. It is essentially a poem to be enjoyed for itself and is not difficult to understand.

What exactly happens in this story?

What words produce sounds which make the story frightening?

Read it aloud, getting louder towards the end of each verse.

Can you think of another object as unpleasant to think about as a Hairy Toe?

For further unpleasantness, see:
    The Knee JV II:67
    The Strange Visitor JV III:63.

The woman scrooched down,
way down under the covers,
and about that time
the wind appeared to hit the house,

smoosh,

and the old house creaked and cracked
like something was trying to get in.
The voice had come nearer,
almost at the door now,
and it said,
'Where's my Hair-r-ry To-o-oe?
Who's got my Hair-r-ry To-o-oe?'

The woman scrooched further down
under the covers
and pulled them tight around her head.

The wind growled around the house
like some big animal
and r-r-um-mbled
over the chimbley.
All at once she heard the door cr-r-a-ack
and Something slipped in
and began to creep over the floor.

The floor went
cre-e-eak, cre-e-eak
at every step that thing took towards her bed.
The woman could almost feel
it bending over her bed.
There in an awful voice it said:
'Where's my Hair-r-ry To-o-oe?
Who's got my Hair-r-ry To-o-oe?
You've got it!'

Traditional American

55

Moon-wind

There is no wind on the moon at all
    Yet things get blown about.
In utter utter stillness
    Your candle shivers out.

In utter utter stillness
    A giant marquee
Booms and flounders past you
    Like a swan at sea.

In utter utter stillness
    While you stand in the street
A squall of hens and cabbages
    Knocks you off your feet.

In utter utter stillness
    While you stand agog
A tearing twisting sheet of pond
    Clouts you with a frog.

A camp of caravans suddenly
    Squawks and takes off.
A ferris wheel bounds along the skyline
    Like a somersaulting giraffe.

Roots and foundations, nails and screws,
    Nothing can hold fast,
Nothing can resist the moon's
    Dead-still blast.

Ted Hughes

Ted Hughes has written many poems about the Moon, using very original **images** to convey the mystery of the Moon. This poem could be studied as an example of a poem of mystery, in the context of the preceding monsters, or as an introduction to several of Hughes' Moon poems.

The poem contains some vivid similes among the images: so an introduction to simile could be made here. (It will be necessary to make sure pupils know what a 'marquee' and a 'ferris wheel' are.)

What is strange about the moon-wind?

There are three different ways in which the poet describes the moon-wind as still. What are they?

How many words can you find in the poem that describe something being blown about?

Read through the poem to yourselves and see where the contrasts between stillness and movement come. Prepare a reading which brings out these contrasts, and read it to the class.

Can you think of any other unlikely effects a moon-wind might have?

For further poems about the Moon and wind, see:

In *The Hag* the rhythm and rhyme convey the **feeling** of strength and speed. The rhythm particularly brings out the movement of the ride of the witch. Read it out to the class, bringing out the relentless rhythm of the lines.

   It will be necessary to make sure the pupils understand the words 'burr', 'brakes', and 'mires'.

What is the hag doing?

What does she look like?

What other frightening things are happening, apart from the hag herself appearing?

When is 'noon of night'?

How many beats are there in each line?

Read the poem again to yourselves carefully, trying to see the rhythm and beat, then chant it all together. [The teacher can give them the beat.]

For a similar tale of witchcraft, see:
   The Turn of the Road JV IV:42
   The Puffin Book of Magic Verse
   Hist Whist.

The Hag

The Hag is astride,
This night for to ride;
The Devil and she together:
Through thick and through thin,
Now out and then in,
Though ne'er so foul be the weather.

A thorn or a burr
She takes for a spur:
With a lash of a bramble she rides now,
Through brakes and through briars,
O'er ditches and mires,
She follows the Spirit that guides now.

No Beast for his food,
Dares now range the wood;
But hushed in his lair he lies lurking:
While mischiefs, by these,
On land and on seas,
At noon of night are a-working.

The storm will arise
And trouble the skies;
This night, and more for the wonder,
The ghost from the tomb
Affrighted shall come,
Called out by the clap of the thunder.

Robert Herrick

A Charm against the Toothache

Venerable Mother Toothache
Climb down from your white battlements,
Stop twisting in your yellow fingers
The fourfold rope of nerves;
And tomorrow I will give you a tot of whisky
To hold in your cupped hands,
A garland of anise-flowers,
And three cloves like nails.

And tell the attendant gnomes
It is time to knock off now,
To shoulder their little pick-axes,
Their cold chisels and drills,
And you may mount by a silver ladder
Into the sky, to grind
In the cracked polished mortar
Of the hollow moon.

By the lapse of warm waters,
And the poppies nodding like red coals,
The paths on the granite mountains,
And the plantation of my dreams.

John Heath-Stubbs

In *A Charm against the Toothache* the **images** used which are associated with teeth and nerves are plentiful and vivid. The feelings evoked by toothache and the very thought of it are emphasized by the images.

What pictures does the poem give of toothache attacking the teeth?

What picture is given of what is happening to the nerves?

Why should he offer whisky, anise flowers, and cloves? What does a clove look like?

What are the gnomes doing? Why does the poet use 'knock off'? (It has two senses here.)

Which words in the poem make you feel the sensation of toothache?

For further charms and spells, see:

JV I:47–49
JV II:64–65;
and throughout *Hist Whist.*

In this poem the **feelings** are evoked more by the regular pattern than by the image. Before reading it to the class, it is important to make sure that the point of the title is understood: that a traveller has been directed the wrong way and is now cursing the ones who gave him the directions. When read aloud, feelings of anger and hatred should be brought out vividly.

What are the various misfortunes that the poet wishes on those who directed him the wrong way?

How many beats are there in each line?

The lines are equal in beats and rhyme in pairs. Read it to yourselves, using the regular beat and rhyme to make it more like a chanted verse. Then chant it together aloud. Make it sound like a curse.

For further curses see *Hist Whist*.

Traveller's Curse After Misdirection

May they stumble, stage by stage
On an endless pilgrimage,
Dawn and dusk, mile after mile,
At each and every step, a stile;
At each and every step withal
May they catch their feet and fall;
At each and every fall they take
May a bone within them break;
And may the bone that breaks within
Not be, for variation's sake,
Now rib, now thigh, now arm, now shin,
But always, without fail, THE NECK.

Robert Graves

Cowboy Song

I come from Salem County
   Where the silver melons grow,
Where the wheat is sweet as an angel's feet
   And the zithering zephyrs blow.
I walk the blue bone-orchard
   In the apple-blossom snow,
When the teasy bees take their honeyed ease
   And the marmalade moon hangs low.

This is a ballad, a poem telling a story. It combines both pattern in the verses and **imagery**. Read it out to the class, bringing out the lazy rhythm of the typical cowboy song.

There are many interesting images to consider, and the next section deals with some of them. But this is a poem to be enjoyed for itself, not just to be treated as a collection of metaphors to be unscrambled.

What unusual or unexpected words are used in the first verse, and what do they mean? For example, what are 'zithering zephyrs' and what is 'apple-blossom snow'?

What is the special effect of the words in line 7 of the first verse?

What has happened to his Ma and Pa?

Where do you first notice or think that the cowboy is dead? When you realize it, are there earlier suggestions that you missed (e.g. bone-orchard)?

Where are the suggestions that he is a ghost haunting the town?

What exactly is meant by 'The bread of my twentieth birthday I buttered with the sun'?

Do you like it as a picture?

What are the last 4 lines of the poem describing? Why is he passing his own coffin?

This poem is called a ballad, which is also a song. Can you think of a simple tune or at least a beat to which to read it (e.g. The Big Rock Candy Mountains)?

For further ballads, and stories, see:
   Pretty Boy Floyd JV IV:37
   The Death of Ned Kelly JV IV:32
   Pibroch JV III:78
   Behind the Hill JV III:67.

My Maw sleeps prone on the prairie
    In a boulder eiderdown,
Where the pickled stars in their little jam-jars
    Hang in a hoop to town.
I haven't seen Paw since a Sunday
    In eighteen seventy-three
When he packed his snap in a bitty mess-trap
    And said he'd be home by tea.

Fled is my fancy sister
    All weeping like the willow,
And dead is the brother I loved like no other
    Who once did share my pillow.
I fly the florid water
    Where run the seven geese round,
O the townsfolk talk to see me walk
    Six inches off the ground.

Across the map of midnight
    I trawl the turning sky,
In my green glass the salt fleets pass
    The moon her fire-float by.
The girls go gay in the valley
    When the boys come down from the farm,
Don't run, my joy, from a poor cowboy,
    I won't do you no harm.

The bread of my twentieth birthday
    I buttered with the sun,
Though I sharpen my eyes with lovers' lies
    I'll never see twenty-one.
Light is my shirt with lilies,
    And lined with lead my hood,
On my face as I pass is a plate of brass,
    And my suit is made of wood.

Charles Causley

Angel Hill

A sailor came walking down Angel Hill,
He knocked on my door with a right good will,
With a right good will he knocked on my door.
He said, 'My friend, we have met before.'
     No, never, said I.

He searched my eye with a sea-blue stare
And he laughed aloud on the Cornish air,
On the Cornish air he laughed aloud
And he said, 'My friend, you have grown too proud.'
     No, never, said I.

This is another ballad. The regular **pattern** of the verses and the repeated 'No, never, said I' make the poem easy to read and add to the persistence shown by the two characters.

It is a poem to be considered on two levels. On the surface it is a tale of two friends meeting after some time and the narrator refusing to recognize the sailor. But at a deeper level there is a suggestion that the sailor represents some inescapable fate. For considering the first level only, the first five points in the next section will suffice. The next three encourage the pursuit of an allegory.

What exactly happens in this story?

What had the sailor and the speaker done together in the war? What exactly is meant by 'vowed our stars should be as one'?

Why do you think the speaker refuses to recognize the sailor?

What does the sailor seem to be asking for?

What sort of message is this story giving about friendship?

What might the sailor mean by 'till you shall give to me my own'?

Why should the sailor think 'You'll send and fetch me one fine day'? And why should he be so contented as he strolls away?

Do you think this sailor is representing something or someone else? (Think about the name of the hill.)

More ballads by Charles Causley are to be found in his *Collected Works*.

For further ballad stories, see:
The Fox JV I:62
The Ballad of Red Fox JV II:55
Samson JV III:85.

'In war we swallowed the bitter bread
And drank of the brine,' the sailor said.
'We took of the bread and we tasted the brine
As I bound your wounds and you bound mine.'
　　No, never, said I.

'By day and night on the diving sea
We whistled to sun and moon,' said he.
'Together we whistled to moon and sun
And vowed our stars should be as one.'
　　No, never, said I.

'And now,' he said, 'that the war is past
I come to your hearth and home at last.
I come to your home and hearth to share
Whatever fortune waits me there.'
　　No, never, said I.

'I have no wife nor son,' he said,
'Nor pillow on which to lay my head,
No pillow have I, nor wife nor son,
Till you shall give to me my own.'
　　No, never, said I.

His eye it flashed like a lightning-dart
And still as a stone then stood my heart.
My heart as a granite stone was still
And he said, 'My friend, but I think you will.'
　　No, never, said I.

The sailor smiled and turned in his track
And shifted the bundle on his back
And I heard him sing as he strolled away,
'You'll send and you'll fetch me one fine day.'
　　No, never, said I.

Charles Causley

Emperors of the Island

There is the story of a deserted island
where five men walked down to the bay.

The story of the island is
that three men would two men slay.

Three men dug two graves in the sand,
three men stood on the sea wet rock,
three shadows moved away.

There is the story of a deserted island
where three men walked down to the bay.

The story of this island is
that two men would one man slay.

Two men dug one grave in the sand,
two men stood on the sea wet rock,
two shadows moved away.

There is the story of a deserted island
where two men walked down to the bay.

The story of this island is
that one man would one man slay.

One man dug one grave in the sand,
one man stood on the sea wet rock,
one shadow moved away.

There is the story of a deserted island
where four ghosts walked down to the bay.

The story of this island is
that four ghosts would one man slay.

Four ghosts dug one grave in the sand,
four ghosts stood on the sea wet rock;
five ghosts moved away.

Dannie Abse

Emperors of the Island is another **story**, but through its imagery it makes the story-line deliberately less obvious. Imagery in poetry produces its effect by implication. Precisely what is happening in this poem is only implied.

The regular pattern of the verse makes it similar to a ballad.

What exactly happens in this story?

Why does the poem have this title?

Read through the poem again to yourselves. It is in sets of three verses. Now read it out aloud in three groups, one group reading the first verse of each set, the next group the second, and the third group the three-line verse of each set.

For further stories with an air of mystery, see:
  The Alice Jean JV I:31
  The Sea Serpent Chantey JV III:24.

The footnote to this poem is important: 'This is a love story from the Middle Ages. The poet obviously knew his subject backwards.' From the title onwards the traditional ingredients of a fairy **story** are reversed, but the poet retains the pattern of regular rhythm and rhyme. Much of the second half can be read with the lines reversed again (i.e. from 'A woodcutter, watching . . .' back to 'The Queen wore the trousers').

Read the poem through to yourselves. What do you notice about the story?
What happens in the story?
Why do you think the poet presented the story in this way?
Think of a really well-known story and write it yourself in reverse, either in verse or prose. For example, you could try a nursery rhyme or one of the story-poems in this book, which have appeared earlier.

For a similar treatment, see *The Story of a Story JV* III:76.

After Ever Happily

or The Princess and the Woodcutter*

And they both lived happily ever after . . .
The wedding was held in the palace. Laughter
Rang to the roof as a loosened rafter
Crashed down and squashed the chamberlain flat –
And how the wedding guests chuckled at that!
'You, with your horny indelicate hands,
Who drop your haitches and call them 'ands,
Who cannot afford to buy her a dress,
How dare you presume to pinch our princess –
Miserable woodcutter, uncombed, unwashed!'
Were the chamberlain's words (before he was squashed).
'Take her,' said the Queen, who had a soft spot
For woodcutters. 'He's strong and he's handsome. Why
    not?'
'What rot!' said the King, but he dare not object;
The Queen wore the trousers – that's as you'd expect.
Said the chamberlain, usually meek and inscrutable,
'A princess and a woodcutter? The match is unsuitable.'
Her dog barked its welcome again and again,
As they splashed to the palace through puddles of rain.
And the princess sighed, 'Till the end of my life!'
'Darling,' said the woodcutter, 'will you be my wife?'
He knew all his days he could love no other,
So he nursed her to health with some help from his
    mother,
And lifted her, horribly hurt, from her tumble.
A woodcutter, watching, saw the horse stumble.
As she rode through the woods, a princess in her prime
On a dapple-grey horse . . . Now, to finish my rhyme,
I'll start it properly: Once upon a time –

* This is a love story from the Middle Ages. The poet obviously knew his
    subject-matter backwards.

Ian Serraillier

First Day at School

A millionbillionwillion miles from home
Waiting for the bell to go. (To go where?)
Why are they all so big, other children?
So noisy? So much at home they
must have been born in uniform
Lived all their lives in playgrounds
Spent the years inventing games
that don't let me in. Games
that are rough, that swallow you up.

And the railings.
All around, the railings.
Are they to keep out wolves and monsters?
Things that carry off and eat children?
Things you don't take sweets from?
Perhaps they're to stop us getting out
Running away from the lessins. Lessin.
What does a lessin look like?
Sounds small and slimy.
They keep them in glassrooms.
Whole rooms made out of glass. Imagine.

I wish I could remember my name
Mummy said it would come in useful.
Like wellies. When there's puddles.
Yellowwellies. I wish she was here.
I think my name is sewn on somewhere
Perhaps the teacher will read it for me.
Tea-cher. The one who makes the tea.

Roger McGough

66

This poem concerns an experience every pupil will know. Before introducing the poem ask them to recall their first day at school at the age of 5. How did they **feel** themselves?
What were their first thoughts about teachers?
What were their first thoughts about the older children?

Now let them read this poem to themselves. Then choose three readers and ask them to read it out to the class, one reader per verse.

Why has he said 'millionbillionwillion miles'? What other very childish words are used?

'Waiting for the bell to go. (To go where?)': this is a school expression new to this child, heard wrong and misunderstood. What other examples of this are there in the poem?

What three points in the first verse show that the child feels strange and alone?

What is unexpected about the child's question about the railings?

What 'don't you take sweets from'?

With 'lessin' the child is trying to find a word-shape, like those on p. 10. Why do you think 'lessin' sounds small and slimy?

The third verse is about grown-ups: mother and teacher. The ideas in the child's head are confused. What is the child trying to remember and think about?

At which point in the poem do you think the child is most nervous?

Now, in groups, prepare a reading of the poem, noting where the nervousness or panic should be brought out. Several groups can read it out in turn (you might make a recording of one of the readings, to a background of playground sounds).

See also:
    Out of School NDBV:118
    The Schoolboy NDBV:116
    A Boy's Head JV IV:79.

This is the story of an incident which will be familiar to many: the moment of uncertainty and then panic. It expresses physical and emotional **feelings** and is similar to the poem *First Day at School* in describing loneliness and insecurity in a situation where others are showing confidence. Read the poem to the class.

What is it they have 'all gone across'?

Why do you think this boy has 'cold feet'? (Is it because he has thought about crossing for too long, while others just did it?)

An 'abyss' is a very deep, dark hole in the ground: why do you think the word is used here?

At what point does the boy start imagining things rather than just feeling things?

Have you ever lost your nerve in any situation or known anyone else do so? Do you think this poem gets the feelings across well?

For other boyish adventures, see:
   Middle Ages JV III:78
   The Apple Tree JV III:67
   Hide and Seek JV IV:70.

Cold Feet

They have all gone across
They are all turning to see
They are all shouting 'come on'
They are all waiting for me.

I look through the gaps in the footway
And my heart shrivels with fear,
For far below the river is flowing
So quick and so cold and so clear.

And all that there is between it
And me falling down there is this:
A few wooden planks – not very thick –
And between each, a little abyss.

The holes get right under my sandals.
I can see straight through to the rocks,
And if I don't look, I can feel it,
Just there, through my shoes and my socks.

Suppose my feet and my legs withered up
And slipped through the slats like a rug?
Suppose I suddenly went very thin
Like the baby that slid down the plug?

I know that it cannot happen
But suppose that it did, what then?
Would they be able to find me
And take me back home again?

They have all gone across
They are all waiting to see
They are all shouting 'come on' —
But they'll have to carry me.

Brian Lee

67

529 1983

Absentmindedly,
sometimes,
I lift the receiver
And dial my own number.

(What revelations,
I think then,
If only
I could get through to myself.)

Gerda Mayer

Rain

The lights are all on, though it's just past midday,
There are no more indoor games we can play,
No one can think of anything to say,
It rained all yesterday, it's raining today,
It's grey outside, inside me it's grey.

I stare out of the window, fist under my chin,
The gutter leaks drips on the lid of the dustbin,
When they say 'cheer up', I manage a grin,
I draw a fish on the glass with a sail-sized fin,
It's sodden outside, and it's damp within.

Matches, bubbles and papers pour into the drains,
Clouds smother the sad laments from the trains,
Grandad says it brings on his rheumatic pains,
The moisture's got right inside of my brains,
It's raining outside, inside me it rains.

Brian Lee

The short poem *529 1983* conveys **feelings** through imagery. The single image of the telephone suggests a broader communication with oneself. It may be necessary to point out the double meaning of 'get through to' as meaning 'to make someone understand' and to 'make contact by telephone'.

What is happening in the poem?
What is a revelation? What verb does it come from?

For similar ideas see *In My New Clothing* JV I:10

In *Rain* the **feelings** of frustration and boredom are conveyed by the repetition of the rhyme, which produces monotony and the image of rain pervading everything inside and out.

Where does the poet show that the rain outside is making the child inside unhappy?
The speaker is staring out of the window: what does he notice about the outside?
Where does he draw his fish?
What other depressing features of being inside on a wet day might the poet have included?
The repeated rhymes bring out how boring the situation is. Read it out so as to show the boring repetition.

For depression pervading everything in a similar way, see *No!* p. 43.

The poem *maggie and millie and molly and may* conveys feelings of involvement and contentment through the imagery of what each of the girls finds on the beach.

What did each of the girls find on the beach?

'As small as a world and as large as alone' is a rather difficult description of a stone. Think hard and suggest what these words mean.

What do you think the poet means by the final line?

What do you enjoy about the sea-side? What particularly would you enjoy there if you were alone?

For further poems about the beach and the sea, see:

pp. 40–41
Seascapes NDBV
The Puffin Book of Salt Sea Verse.

---

maggie and millie and molly and may
went down to the beach (to play one day)

and maggie discovered a shell that sang
so sweetly she couldn't remember her troubles, and

milly befriended a stranded star
whose rays five languid fingers were;

and molly was chased by a horrible thing
which raced sideways while blowing bubbles; and

may came home with a smooth white stone
as small as a world and as large as alone.

For whatever we lose (like a you or a me)
it's always ourselves we find in the sea

e. e. cummings

Horrible Song

The Crow is a wicked creature
    Crooked in every feature.
Beware, beware of the Crow!
When the bombs burst, he laughs, he shouts;
When guns go off, he roundabouts;
When the limbs start to fly and the blood starts to flow
    Ho Ho Ho
    He sings the Song of the Crow.

If you are working through the book page by page, there is a big jump from *maggie and millie and molly and may* to *Horrible Song*. This poem needs to be read out to emphasize the gloating, triumphant, almost small-boyish **feeling** in it. It is excellent for mixed chorus and solo reading.

Do you like this crow?
What sort of creature is he?
Do you ever share his pleasure in doing wrong?
Which group of words gives you the best picture of him?

Follow-up poems on birds are listed together, facing page 73.

The Crow is a sudden creature
    Thievish in every feature.
Beware, beware of the Crow!
When the sweating farmers sleep
He levers the jewels from the heads of their sheep.
Die in a ditch, your own will go,
    Ho Ho Ho
    While he sings the Song of the Crow.

The Crow is a subtle creature
    Cunning in every feature.
Beware, beware of the Crow!
When sick folk tremble on their cots
He sucks their souls through the chimney pots,
They're dead and gone before they know,
    Ho Ho Ho
    And he sings the Song of the Crow.

The Crow is a lusty creature
    Gleeful in every feature.
Beware, beware of the Crow!
If he can't get your liver, he'll find an old rat
Or highway hedgehog hammered flat,
Any old rubbish to make him grow,
    Ho Ho Ho
    While he sings the Song of the Crow.

The Crow is a hardy creature
    Fire-proof in every feature.
Beware, beware of the Crow!
When Mankind's blasted to kingdom come
The Crow will dance and hop and drum
And into an old thigh-bone he'll blow
    Ho Ho Ho
    Singing the Song of the Crow.

Ted Hughes

Robin

With a bonfire throat,
Legs of twig
A dark brown coat,
The inspector robin
Comes where I dig.

Military man
With a bright eye
And a wooden leg,
He must scrounge and beg
Now the summer's by:

Beg at the doors,
Scrounge in the gardens,
While daylight lessens
And the grass glistens
And the ground hardens.

The toads have their vaults,
The squirrels their money,
The swifts their journey:
For him the earth's anger,
The taste of hunger.

And his unfrightened song
For the impending snows
Is also for the rose,
And for the great armada
And the Phoenician trader,
And the last missile raider –
It's the only one he knows.

Hal Summers

Robins are familiar from Christmas cards and most people's back gardens. The first two-and-a-half verses of this poem are full of attractive, easily imitated, **imagery.** The second half is more difficult to understand. Specific examples are used to convey abstract ideas.

---

*In the first verse he has 'Legs of twig' and in the second 'a wooden leg'.
Why is each one used in its verse?*

Which one do you prefer?

Do you prefer 'inspector robin' or 'Military man'?

In verse 4 what is the earth's anger? What is the taste of hunger?

What does the writer feel about the robin?

See the next page for more poems about birds.

Although this shares the same subject as *Horrible Song* it is so different that it would be a mistake to link them as two poems about crows. This poem makes explicit the link between the **images** in dreams and their counterparts in the real world.

What exactly did the writer really see?
What picture did he get in his imagination?
Is his crow anything like Ted Hughes's?
In what ways are the crows different in the two poems?

Other bird poems in *Junior Voices*:
    Feel Like a Bird II:52
    The Starlings in George Square IV:10;
and pages 65 to 74 in *NDBV*;
for imagery, *The Locust JV* III:13;
for ways of looking at things,
    Elephants are different to Different People JV III:17.

Night Crow

When I saw that clumsy crow
Flap from a wasted tree,
A shape in the mind rose up:
Over the gulfs of dream
Flew a tremendous bird
Further and further away
Into a moonless black,
Deep in the brain, far back.

Theodore Roethke

October garden:
At the top of the tree
A thrush stabs an apple.

November Story

The evening had caught cold;
Its eyes were blurred.
It had a dripping nose
And its tongue was furred.

I sat in a warm bar
After the day's work;
November snuffled outside,
Greasing the sidewalk.

But soon I had to go
Out into the night
Where shadows prowled the alleys,
Hiding from the light.

But light shone at the corner
On the pavement where
A man had fallen over
Or been knocked down there.

His legs on the slimed concrete
Were splayed out wide;
He had been propped against a lamp-post;
His head lolled to one side.

A victim of crime or accident,
An image of fear,
He remained quite motionless
As I drew near.

Then a thin voice startled silence
From a doorway close by
Where an urchin hid from the wind:
'Spare a penny for the guy!'

These two poems are obviously best read close to November 5th.
They are both rich in **images,** as fits a day that is so rich in sense
impressions.

What happens in this poem?

What is the weather like?

Which group of words about the weather do you like best?

Which group of words about the guy do you like best?

Write a riddle about a guy.

This is a simple poem with one sustained **image**. You may feel that the first half of the second verse isn't as good as the rest of the poem.

In what ways are fireworks like flowers?
In what ways are they different?
Does the word 'showers' in the third line fit in with the picture of flowers?
Write a riddle about a firework.

Poems on fireworks and guys are absent from *JV* and *NDBV*. There are short lists on both in *Where's That Poem?*

But see *No!* on page 40.

I gave the boy some money
And hastened on.
A voice called, 'Thank you guv'nor!'
And the words upon

The wincing air seemed strange –
So hoarse and deep –
As if the guy had spoken
In his restless sleep.

Vernon Scannell

Fireworks

They rise like sudden fiery flowers
  That burst upon the night,
Then fall to earth in burning showers
  Of crimson, blue, and white.

Like buds too wonderful to name,
  Each miracle unfolds,
And catherine-wheels begin to flame
  Like whirling marigolds.

Rockets and Roman candles make
  An orchard of the sky,
Whence magic trees their petals shake
  Upon each gazing eye.

James Reeves

November Morning:
A whiff of cordite
Caught in the leaf mould.

Carol

The Palm Court Lounge is snug and warm
There's Scotch on every table
It's not our fault it's not so hot
Next door in the hotel stable

The passengers are drunk tonight
The crew have cash to burn
So who will hear the drowning man
We've left ten miles astern?

Let's all go down the Motorway
And see who's first at Chester
Let's all forget that scruffy dog
We knocked for six at Leicester

O we're all right and so is Jack
(He's underneath the table)
It's not our fault it's not so hot
Next door in the hotel stable

God rest us merry, Gentlemen,
This is no time for sorrow
Because ten thousand refugees
Will get no grub tomorrow

The Landlord smiles and lays the bill
Quite gently on the table
The man who'll pay has just been born
Next door in an ice-cold stable.

Ronald Deadman

76

Carol treads the narrow way between self-awareness and self-righteousness. This kind of Morality needs careful handling. The various **images** all lead to the same feeling.

What is happening in each verse?

Is there one feeling that all the people in the poem share?

What do you feel about these people?

The Computer's First Christmas Card is a deservedly well-anthologized poem. It earns its place, despite its familiarity, because it is the best example of its kind of **pattern** poem. Any reading should try to give a computer-like effect.

Which of the lines that seem to be nonsense in fact make some sense?

Why is the poem this shape on the page?

Does it capture any of the sounds of Christmas?

Other Edwin Morgan poems:
    Endless Chant JV I:79
    Orgy JV III:23;
Other Christmas poems:
    Journey of the Magi NDBV:225
    and the whole of *A Single Star.*

The Computer's First Christmas Card

jollymerry
hollyberry
jollyberry
merryholly
happyjolly
jollyjelly
jellybelly
bellymerry
hollyheppy
jollyMolly
marryJerry
merryHarry
hoppyBarry
heppyJarry
boppyheppy
berryjorry
jorryjelly
moppyjelly
Mollymerry
Jerryjolly
bellyboppy
jorryhoppy
hollymoppy
Barrymerry
Jarryhappy
happyboppy
boppyjolly
jollymerry
merrymerry
merrymerry
merryChris
asmerryasa
Chrismerry
asMERRYCHR
YSANTHEMUM

Edwin Morgan

TV

In the coloured world of home
there's a greyish oblong hole;
and it's the only thing that
moves among the furniture.

Somewhere past the couch tiny
clouds and horses spring into
view and disappear before
they get to the window-sill.

Though these things and beings are
so small, their noise is human.
Passing empty rooms, you hear
gun-shots and angry talking.

Even when there is no one
to see or hear it, this life
in the curved glass probably
goes on just the same. Who knows?

Our universe began in
a concentrated atom.
So does this screen of shadows
when you first switch on the knob.

It also ends like that as
you switch the other way, though
first the sound dies, and all yell,
but cannot make themselves heard.

Roy Fuller

Postscript on the arrival of colour

In the greyish world of home
there's a coloured oblong hole;
and naturally we all sit
with our red eyes glued on it.

This poem links up with *Steam Shovel* on page 36 and with *My Father* on page 48. Its **images** lead into the fantasy. Note how carefully observed it is.

What programme is on the TV?

Does the programme go on if there is no one to see or hear it?

Look at Verse 4: *Write a few lines about a radio set in the same way.*

Verse 5 is about the beginning of the world and the moment when you first switch on the set. Verse 6 is about the moment when you switch off. Why does the author compare it with the end of the world?

Do you like the first verse or the Postscript best? Which best describes the TV set in the home?

What else can you call a Television Set?

Compare:
    The Door JV IV:2
and Ted Hughes's *Public Bar TV* in *Wodwo* (Faber paperback).

This poem provides a good contrast to *TV*. It too uses **images** to make its points. You may think that it presents too romantic a picture of country childhood, while *TV* presents the worst of television watching, and that there is an unfair comparison here. The pupils' questions could lead to a discussion of this.
(mixen = dungheap)

Why does the writer say that both the farm child's head and his pockets are stuffed with things?

Why do you think the 'thorn and thistle tuft' are mentioned?

Why does the poem end with 'the stubborn plough'? or
Why does the earth beckon *to the stubborn plough?*

Which group of words gives you the best picture of the farm child?

In TV *there is a child indoors. What could you say his head was stuffed with?*

The farm child has a harebell hiding in his eyes. What does this mean? What might the child be watching TV have in his?

Which child is most like you?

A similar poem is *A Boy's Head JV* IV:79. This provides a good model for writing.
See also *An Ordinary Day JV* IV:3.
The other side of the case is presented in R. S. Thomas's *Welsh Hill Country NDBV*:20.

Farm Child

Look at this village boy, his head is stuffed
With all the nests he knows, his pockets with flowers,
Snail-shells and bits of glass, the fruit of hours
Spent in the fields by thorn and thistle tuft.
Look at his eyes, see the harebell hiding there;
Mark how the sun has freckled his smooth face
Like a finch's egg under that bush of hair
That dares the wind, and in the mixen now
Notice his poise: from such unconscious grace
Earth breeds and beckons to the stubborn plough.

R. S. Thomas

My Bonny Black Bess

Dick Turpin bold! Dick, hie away,
Was the cry of my pals, who were startled, I guess,
For the pistols were levelled, the bullets whizzed by,
As I leapt on the back of Black Bess.
Three Officers mounted, led forward the chase,
Resolv'd in the capture to share;
But I smil'd on their efforts, tho' swift was their pace,
As I urg'd on my bonny Black Mare.
So when I've a bumper, what can I do less,
   Than the memory drink of my bonny Black Bess?

Hark away, hark away! still onward they press,
As we saw by the glimmer of morn,
Tho' many a mile on the back of Black Bess,
That night I was gallantly borne;
Hie over, my pet, the fatigue I must bear
Well clear'd! never falter for breath,
Hark forward, my girl, my bonny Black Mare,
We speed it for life or for death.
But when I've a bumper, what can I do less,
   Than the memory drink of my bonny Black Bess?

The spires of York now burst on my view,
But the chimes, they were ringing her knell,
Halt! Halt! my brave mare, they no longer pursue,
She halted, she staggered, she fell!
Her breathing was o'er, all was hushed as the grave,
Alas! poor Black Bess, once my pride,
Her heart she had burst, her rider to save,
For Dick Turpin, she lived, and she died.
Then the memory drink of my bonny Black Bess,
Hurrah for poor bonny Black Bess!

Anon

This ballad celebrates the heroic death of a horse. Modern sympathies are likely to be indignantly on the horse's side. The **story** is the important thing. It would be best to explain 'bumper' before reading the poem.

What exactly is happening in each verse?
What else do you know about Dick Turpin?
Does this poem have enough information in it for you to understand it?
Is this poem more difficult to understand than the others you have read in this book? If it is, what makes it so?

Other story poems:
    How Samson Bore away the Gates of Gaza JV III:85
    The Highwayman NDBV:140;
and an interesting idea:
    Cowboys NDBV:139.

Reindeer

I wriggled silently through the swamp,
carrying bow and arrow in my mouth.
The marsh was broad, the water icy cold,
and there was no cover in sight.

Slowly, soaked, invisible,
I crawled within range.
The reindeer were eating;
they grazed the juicy moss
without concern,
till my arrow sank
tremblingly deep
into the bull's side.

Terrified, the unsuspecting herd
hastily scattered,
and vanished at the sharpest trot
to shielding hills.

Aua

The Mouse's Invitation Cards

'Come at seven,' 'Come at nine,'
'Come whenever you want.'
On the shelf the printed cards
Seem kind in their intent.

But the mouse will always stay at home,
He will never venture out,
No matter how the cards insist
Friends are all about.

This is a group of three poems about hunting and being hunted. In them the use of **images** arouses feelings in the reader. It is probably best to read and discuss them together. *Reindeer* is a realistic picture, sympathetic to the hunter, while the other two are in the Aesop's Fables tradition, using a story to point a moral.

What makes you sorry for the hunter in Reindeer?
Why does he say that the arrow sank 'tremblingly' deep?
Did he succeed in his hunt?
How would you write this to make a reader sorry for the reindeer?

What is the moral of The Mouse's Invitation Cards? *Does it have a message for you?*
Is this about real mice at all?

For *Reindeer*, see *Eskimo Hunting Song* JV III:54.
For *The Mouse's Invitation Cards*, see *The Meadow Mouse* JV IV:15.

Do you think that the last two lines of The Owl's Trick *are the most horrible?*
How like a human cattle-farm is the owl's mouse-farm?
Which pictures in the poem are most unpleasant?

Which of these three poems do you like best?
In what order would you choose to read them out?
Practise reading them to gain the best effect.

The Owl's Trick, see *Town Owl NDBV*:65.
And for this group:
  King of Beasts JV IV:13
  The Fox JV I:62
  Pike NDBV:60.

One's from a cat, one's from an owl,
And both are intent
To draw him from his nest and then
Have him where they want.

Brian Patten

The Owl's Trick

In a place, dark, disguised,
A place not fit for our eyes,
In a hollow, ancient tree
The owl speaks philosophically:

'About my feet are swarms of mice
And I can easily leave them there.
From their feet I've ripped their toes,
And now they'll not go anywhere.

'I eat them slowly at my ease,
I pick and choose them as I please.
The fattest one I let digest
Before indulging in the next.

'I bring them corn into my croft,
It keeps them alive and it keeps them soft.
Before this idea came to me
They were nimble and ran away.

'Now I've neatly torn the paws from each
And they panic forever within my reach.
This trick mankind viewed with alarm –
And then invented the Cattle-farm.'

Brian Patten

The Game of Life

Have you been in sight of heaven
Far ahead on ninety-seven,
Then swirled the dice and thrown a one,
Slid down a snake and flopped upon
Some square like sixty-three?

And then what made you even madder
Seen your sister climb a ladder
To eighty-four from twenty-eight
And felt a sudden rush of hate
As she smirked with glee?

And have you thought she counted out
(So as to miss a snake's dread snout)
A few too many squares – and stayed
Quiet because you were afraid
Or just through leniency?

If so, you will already know
How bitter life can be; and show
Upon your countenance no sign
Except perhaps a smile benign.
And shake on doggedly.

Roy Fuller

The Game of Life uses a simple comparison to discuss complex **feelings** about others, and especially brothers and sisters. There is an opportunity here to copy the idea and apply it to other games.

What happens in the first verse?
What feeling does this give the player?
What exactly happens in the third verse?
What two feelings are mentioned in that verse?
Can you think of times when life itself has been like the game?
What in real life would be shaking on doggedly?

For the struggles of life, see the opposite page.

This poem develops the use of a real event to discuss **feelings** about an abstract idea. It can be read just as a description of an event.

Read the first three lines of the second verse and the last line but one. Why did he choose the road he went along?

Now read the last two lines of the second verse and the first two of the third verse? Do these agree with the first group?

How, then, do you think he chose which way to go?

Do you think he is glad or sorry he went that way?

The writer is using the picture of the two roads to talk about his own life. What do you think he is saying about it?

Very similar is Frost's *Acquainted with the Night* NDBV:229.
See also:
    The Way through the Woods NDBV:18
    Uphill NDBV:227.

The Road not Taken

Two roads diverged in a yellow wood,
And sorry I could not travel both
And be one traveller, long I stood
And looked down one as far as I could
To where it bent in the undergrowth;

Then took the other, as just as fair,
And having perhaps the better claim,
Because it was grassy and wanted wear;
Though as for that the passing there
Had worn them really about the same,

And both that morning equally lay
In leaves no step had trodden black.
Oh, I kept the first for another day!
Yet knowing how way leads on to way,
I doubted if I should ever come back.

I shall be telling this with a sigh
Somewhere ages and ages hence:
Two roads diverged in a wood, and I –
I took the one less travelled by,
And that has made all the difference.

Robert Frost

The Apple-raid

Darkness came early, though not yet cold;
Stars were strung on the telegraph wires;
Street lamps spilled pools of liquid gold;
The breeze was spiced with garden fires.

That smell of burnt leaves, the early dark,
Can still excite me but not as it did
So long ago when we met in the park –
Myself, John Peters and David Kidd.

We moved out of town to the district where
The lucky and wealthy had their homes
With garages, gardens, and apples to spare
Ripely clustered in the trees' green domes.

We chose the place we meant to plunder
And climbed the wall and dropped down to
The secret dark. Apples crunched under
Our feet as we moved through the grass and dew.

The clusters on the lower boughs of the tree
Were easy to reach. We stored the fruit
In pockets and jerseys until all three
Boys were heavy with their tasty loot.

Safe on the other side of the wall
We moved back to town and munched as we went.
I wonder if David remembers at all
That little adventure, the apples' fresh scent.

Strange to think that he's fifty years old,
That tough little boy with scabs on his knees;
Stranger to think that John Peters lies cold
In an orchard in France beneath apple trees.

Vernon Scannell

86

The pupil's book ends with a group of five fairly long poems telling **stories.** It may be best, if you have worked through from the beginning, to read and talk about them without using the questions provided.

The Apple-raid relates a simple **story**, which it then twists in the last verse to evoke strong feelings.

How many senses (sight, hearing, touch, smell, taste) are used in this poem?

Which one do you think is most important in this poem?

There are two places where the pace of the story changes. They match the places where it shifts from the present day to the writer's childhood. Where are they?

How would you mark this change when you read the poem aloud?

What happened to John Peters?

Why does the writer save this for the last two lines?

Suitable poems to read with this would be *By St Thomas Water NDBV:95;*
and with the first part of *The Apple-raid: The Squad Car JV* I:33.

While *The Apple-raid* sounds true, this poem is one we would like to be true. It, too, is concerned with loss in war but this time we are concerned by the first two lines. Its **story** is told in scenes.

This poem has three scenes, like a play. What happens in each one?
Why do the last three lines come back to the Spitfire?
What differences are there between the marbles and the Spitfire scenes?
What words give you the best picture of Uncle Harry?

For three variations on the ideas in this poem, see:
    Uncle Jack JV III:42
    Snakecharmer NDBV:148
    Welsh Incident NDBV:212.

The Spitfire on the Northern Line

Harry was an uncle. I saw him twice.
Both times he was a sailor home from war.
First, he arrived one morning, thumped the door,
Annoying old Ma Brown on the second floor,
And brought me two string-bags click-full of marbles.
In the grey light of that wartime dawn we lay
On the cold lino, rumbling zig-zag balls
Of colour to all corners of the room,
Until Ma Brown banged up at us with her broom.
I felt like a god in heaven, playing with thunder.
The second time, we went by Underground
To see his mother, my grandma. In all
That packed and rocking tube-train; down we sat
Together on the dirty wooden slats
Between the feet of passengers, and began
To build a Spitfire. He would send me off
Toddling with tininess against the sway
Of the train to fetch a propeller, then the wheels,
While like a Buddha crosslegged, all in blue,
He sat and bashed a nail or sank a screw.
And before the eyes of all, a Spitfire grew
And finally (a stop before the Angel)
He cried 'It's finished!' and the whole coachful
Shouted 'Hooray!'
                          Never, never again
Did I see Harry. Somewhere he was killed
And they slipped his body softly to the sea.
Thousands died that war. Most, like Harry,
Not distinguished by the enemies gunned down,
But remembered by some child.
                                        I see it still,
That Spitfire on the Northern Line, nose-up,
Blotched with its camouflage, and gleaming bright,
And all those faces laughing with delight.

Brian James

The Rescue

The boy climbed up into the tree.
The tree rocked; so did he.
He was trying to rescue a cat,
A cushion of a cat, from where it sat
In a high crutch of branches, mewing
As though to say to him, 'Nothing doing,'

Whenever he shouted, 'Come on, come down.'
So up he climbed, and the whole town
Lay at his feet, round him the leaves
Fluttered like a lady's sleeves,
And the cat sat, and the wind blew so
That he would have flown had he let go.
At last he was high enough to scoop
That fat white cushion or nincompoop
And tuck her under his arm, and turn
To go down –
                    But oh! he began to learn
How high he was, how hard it would be
Having come up with four limbs, to go down with three.
His heart-beats knocked as he tried to think:
He would put the cat in a lower chink –
She appealed to him with a cry of alarm
And put her eighteen claws in his arm.
So he stayed looking down for a minute or so
To the good ground so far below.
When the minute started he saw it was hard;
When it ended he couldn't move a yard.

The Rescue tells a **story** and highlights the accompanying feelings. It has clear visual pictures, but you may feel it lacks the sense of the touch of the tree or the force of the wind.

What exactly happens in this story?

The boy's feelings change several times. What different feelings does he have? What words mark his change of feelings?

How would you read it aloud to make clear where the action and his feelings change?

The poem could have ended two lines earlier. What do the last two lines add?

Which senses are used in this poem? Which is the most important in it?

After this you must read Kit Wright's *Dad and the Cat and the Tree* in *Rabbiting On* for a funny treatment of the same idea.

To match the serious note:

  The Way to the Boiler was Dark JV III:71
  Cornish Holiday NDBV:50.

So there he was stuck, in the failing light
And the wind rising with the coming of the night.
His father! He shouted for all he was worth.
His father came nearer: 'What on earth –?'
'I've got the cat up here but I'm stuck.'
'Hold on. . . . ladder . . .', he heard. Oh, luck!
How lovely behind the branches tossing
The globes at the pedestrian crossing
And the big fluorescent lamps glowed
Mauve-green on the main road.
But his father didn't come back, didn't come;
His little fingers were going numb.

The cat licked them as though to say
'Are you feeling cold? I'm O.K.'
He wanted to cry, he would count ten first,
But just as he was ready to burst,
A torch came and his father and mother
And a ladder and the dog and his younger brother.
Up on a big branch stood his father,
His mother came to the top of the ladder,
His brother stood on a lower rung,
The dog sat still and put out its tongue.
From one to another the cat was handed
And afterwards she was reprimanded.
After that it was easy, though the wind blew:
The parents came down, the boy came too
From the ladder, the lower branch and the upper
And all of them went indoors to supper,
And the tree rocked and the moon sat
In the branches like a white cat.

Hal Summers

Late Home

I looked up – the sun had gone down
Though it was there a minute before
And the light had grown terribly thin
And no one played by the shore
Of the lake, now empty, and still;
And I heard the park-keepers shout
As they cycled around the paths . . .
'Closing, closing . . . everyone out . . . '

Then I panicked and started to run,
Leaving all of my friends behind
(I could hear their cries in the bushes –
It was me they were trying to find)
But they had the burn and the minnows,
The rope, the slide, the shrubbery track,
And the trees where a thrush was singing,
And I had the long road back –

The road that led, empty and straight,
Down under the tall grey flats
Where the lights were on, and the tellies,
And old ladies were putting out cats:
I ran past them, without looking round
As though I'd committed a crime:
At six they'd said 'Just half an hour'
And *now* – oh, what was the time?

How could it have gone already?
Something must be, it *must* be, wrong –
I've only just come out – and why
Does getting back take me so long?
I can't be late – or if I am,
It's the fault of the sun or the moon.
When the dentist's takes an eternity,
How are happy things over so soon?

Late Home deals with **feelings** of panic and reflection. It needs a good reading to mark the changes of pace.

What exactly happens in this poem?

Which parts deal with panic, which with milder worry, and which with happiness?

Choose one picture from the poem for each of these feelings.

Do you remember a similar occasion? Were your feelings like those in the poem?

Hard Cheese JV III:68 is an excellent partner for this.
See also: *Hide and Seek* NDBV:99, JV IV:70;
and perhaps *False Security* NDBV:120;
and compare with *Cold Feet* on page 67.

So I stopped and asked, 'Please mister ... '
And his left wrist came slowly round
And he peered at his watch and shook it
And said 'Blast, it's never been wound up.'
But the next man hauled his watch up,
Like a lead sinker on a line,
Clicked open the front, and boomed out,
'Right now, child, it's five to nine'.

There's a great big gap in between
The way things are, the way things seem,
And I dropped down it then, like you do
When you shoot back to life from a dream.
I stood there and muttered 'It can't be –
His watch must be wrong' – then, aghast –
'This time, I'll *really* be for it.
If it isn't a whole two hours fast.'

But I got my legs going again
And ran, gulping in red-hot air,
Through back-streets where no one knew me,
Till I came out in the Town Square.
But when I looked at the shining face
And I heard the cheerful chimes
Of the Town Hall clock – then every hope
Drained away, as it struck nine times.

Two hours late ... two hours late –
Perhaps they've called out the police
Two hours late ... who, all in a line,
Are combing the waste ground, piece by piece;
While *they* all stand in our window
Anxious and angry and, when I'm seen,
Ready to frown and shout 'There he is',
'Come here you!', and 'Where's the child been?'

When I come round the corner and see them,
I'll limp, as though I'd a sprain,
Then whimper 'I didn't mean it' and
'I'll never ever go out, again . . .
How can I know that time's up,
When I'm enjoying myself such a lot?
I'm sorry – won't you take me back in?
Are you glad to see me, or not?'

. . . But later in bed, as I lay there
In the extraordinary light –
Filtering through the half-drawn curtain –
Of that silvery spellbound night,
I wondered just what *had* happened
To Time, for three hours in June:
If all of my life is as happy –
Will it all be over as soon?

Brian Lee

Legend is a poem that uses bright pictures and the framework of a quest adventure story to convey a feeling. The title should probably be discussed before the poem is read. Be careful not to spoil the overall effect by asking too many questions about individual phrases.

What feeling do you get when the poem is read to you?
Read it slowly to yourself and see if you feel the same.
Do the blacksmith's boy's feelings change during the poem?
Which group of words do you like best?
Can you remember a time when you felt like this?

The perfect follow-up, although more difficult, is *Fern Hill* NDBV:93.
See also:
    The Collier JV IV:90.

Legend

The blacksmith's boy went out with a rifle
and a black dog running behind.
Cobwebs snatched at his feet,
rivers hindered him,
thorn branches caught at his eyes to make him blind
and the sky turned into an unlucky opal,
but he didn't mind,
I can break branches, I can swim rivers, I can stare out any
    spider I meet,
said he to his dog and his rifle.

The blacksmith's boy went over the paddocks
with his old black hat on his head.
Mountains jumped in his way,
rocks rolled down on him,
and the old crow cried, You'll soon be dead.
And the rain came down like mattocks.
But he only said
I can climb mountains, I can dodge rocks, I can shoot an
    old crow any day,
and he went on over the paddocks.

When he came to the end of the day the sun began falling.
Up came the night ready to swallow him,
like the barrel of the gun,
like an old black hat,
like a black dog hungry to follow him.
Then the pigeon, the magpie and the dove began wailing
and the grass lay down to billow him.
His rifle broke, his hat flew away and his dog was gone
and the sun was falling.

But in front of the night the rainbow stood on a mountain,
just as his heart foretold.
He ran like a hare,
he climbed like a fox;
he caught it in his hands, the colour and the cold –
like a bar of ice, like the column of a fountain,

like a ring of gold.
The pigeon, the magpie and the dove flew to stare,
And the grass stood up again on the mountain.

The blacksmith's boy hung the rainbow on his shoulder
instead of his broken gun.
Lizards ran out to see,
snakes made way for him,
and the rainbow shone as brightly as the sun.
All the world said, Nobody is braver, nobody is bolder,
Nobody else has done
anything to equal it. He went home as bold as he could be
with the swinging rainbow on his shoulder.

Judith Wright

Index of Titles and First Lines

Oxford University Press, Walton Street, Oxford OX2 6DP

Oxford   London   Glasgow   New York   Toronto   Melbourne   Wellington   Kuala Lumpur   Singapore
Jakarta   Hong Kong   Tokyo   Delhi   Bombay   Calcutta   Madras   Karachi   Nairobi · Dar es Salaam
Cape Town

Selection and arrangement

© Oxford University Press, 1979   ISBN 0 19 834266 7

Set, printed and bound in Great Britain by
Fakenham Press Limited, Fakenham, Norfolk